A Traveller's Guide
to the Journey

A Traveller's Guide to the Journey

*An Inspirational and Devotional
Guide to Life's Journey*

CHRISTOPHER TINGLE

authorHOUSE®

AuthorHouse™
1663 Liberty Drive
Bloomington, IN 47403
www.authorhouse.com
Phone: 1-800-839-8640

First published by AuthorHouse   September 24th 2011

ISBN: 978-1-4670-0063-5 (sc)
ISBN: 978-1-4670-0062-8 (ebk)

Printed in the United States of America

Contents

＊ ＊ ＊ ＊ ＊ ＊ ＊ ＊ ＊ ＊ ＊ ＊ ＊

Dedication

THIS BOOK IS DEDICATED TO many people but firstly I want to mention two men who have had a great impact on my life but sadly they have completed this life's Journey and have already entered Chapter 13 of this book.

The first is Rev. Michael P. Everson, who, as my Pastor, believed in me, encouraged me, and gave me opportunities to shine that I didn't always do justice to, but hopefully he will somehow get pleasure out of the knowledge of where I have come in my own Journey. Though he is no longer with us he is still much appreciated.

The second is someone else who left this world before I finished this book, Brian Klemmer, a man whose life work has enabled me to experience some amazing things as I have embarked on a Journey of doing the Klemmer and Associates training seminars. This book is the fruit of the last of those seminars, Samurai Camp, of which I am a graduate.

It is also dedicated to my darling wife Desley, who always believed in me far more than I ever believed in myself, and has been a wonderful companion and partner on our life's Journey of over 34 years together now, and to my six children who have always supported and loved me and encouraged me in my literary efforts. Desley is also largely responsible for designing the cover, for which she has not only my thanks but my utmost admiration.

Of course I also wish to honour and thank my dad and mum who started me on the earthly part of my journey and did a pretty good job of bringing me up because I think I turned out all right!

Thanks also to my Pastor, Lesley Everson who has demonstrated that life's Journey doesn't come to an end just because things don't go the way we planned and to the members of our church who have always responded positively to the messages I have preached.

Lastly thanks go to all the wonderful people in Samurai Camp 21 who encouraged and supported me during the writing of this book, especially my buddy Wayne, who helped me to see that this book was so important for me to write.

Thank you all, and enjoy the Journey with me!

Introduction

C ONFUCIUS IS REPORTED TO HAVE said "A Journey of a thousand miles begins with a single step". Actually he wasn't quite right. A Journey of any kind starts with a decision—a choice. When I woke up this morning I was not intending to start this book—which is a kind of Journey within a Journey. The Journey I have been on in my life has led me to this point. It's not a destination, it's just a waypoint, but at this waypoint I begin another Journey within my Journey while carrying on with my original Journey. I'm probably not making a lot of sense, but I trust that as you read on you will be blessed by what follows, because I don't want the fruits of my Journeying to be in vain.

I like to walk and talk. I used to have long discussions with my brother walking our dog, when we would solve the problems of the world together. It is my prayer that this will be my way of walking with you and talking as we are walking and that somewhere during that Journey you will find something to help you as you go along. I don't know where you are in your Journey. But the point is that you are on it, and while you are on it, you sometimes feel like you are walking alone. Perhaps for a short while I can help relieve that loneliness.

Others of you are lost. You keep going, but you don't know where you are coming from or going to. Maybe this book will be a kind of map to you—not to get you to your destination, but to get you back to someplace that's familiar. That's usually enough to get you on track again. Lost is not a good place to be and we all look for something familiar when we don't know where we are. My Journey has probably intersected with yours at some stage, so look out for something you recognise!

I don't mean for this to be an overtly religious book, but one of my travelling companions on my Journey is Jesus. You'll be hearing about Him from time to time and He will influence the story. If you don't know Him, then that's fine, just treat Him as you would anyone who was also walking with a friend—you will get to know Him a bit along the way and you may want to get to know Him better. I do mean, however for this to be a deeply spiritual book, because only at that level is communication meaningful.

I hope you'll also get to meet someone else very important on this Journey too: yourself. I only recently got to know myself in a new way and found a person I liked. Not liking yourself is a drab way to live life, but many of us do it and just think it's normal. I don't know about normal, but it isn't necessary. You are somebody that the world deserves to know, whether they realise it or not, and as you get to know and like yourself better, you won't mind introducing yourself to us a bit more often.

So get out your back pack, your best hiking boots, some appropriate clothing and some snacks and drinks for the way, and let's get started on our Journey.

Under a Tree

❖ ❖ ❖ ❖ ❖ ❖ ❖ ❖ ❖ ❖ ❖ ❖ ❖

ALL JOURNEYS HAVE TO HAVE a beginning and life is no exception. One day you were in a place that was warm, comfortable, dark and a bit cramped, but basically safe. Then after a lot of noise and pushing, you found yourself in a much more spacious place, but the lights were blinding, the temperature was up and down all the time, and people kept poking at you. You won't remember any of it, of course, but that was the first day of your life as an independent person, the day of your birth.

The circumstances of your birth may have affected you deeply. Were you born rich or poor? Did you have a physical affliction that you either got over or is still with you? Were you born one gender and either think you should have been or wish you were, born the other (be thankful there are only two)? Were you discarded or nearly discarded shortly after your birth? We'll get to that part of your Journey later; I am thinking of a beginning that is earlier than that.

Depending on your viewpoint, your life actually started around nine months (or maybe significantly less for some of you) before your birth. At the moment your father's sperm fertilised your mother's egg, something magical happened, and the process of creating your body began. Some of you believe you became a person at that point also, but leaving that aside, at the very least this represents another beginning of life for you.

So did the circumstances of your conception have any bearing on you at all? You may have been born of a loving, committed relationship between two wonderful people, but perhaps you think of yourself as a product of less than favourable conditions in that regard. Maybe a rape was involved, or maybe you were just a child born to fulfil the requirement for an heir. Some people think of themselves as just a drunken accident. "I am a bottle of whisky," I have heard one person say. The possibility even exists these days that you were the result of an anonymous donation of sperm. As tragic as some of this may seem, we are not at this point of the Journey yet because we are still not at the beginning I am looking for.

Even before your birth, circumstances were afoot that were going to affect your future. That conception was never going to take place unless a man and a woman came together. What sort of people were they? What sort of families did they have? What were their attitudes to having children? Believe it or not, that comment about being a twinkle in your mother and father's eyes has more meaning that we give it credit for. In a sense you existed before you existed. People were thinking about you before there was a you to think about.

Did your mother and father desperately want a child, and were delighted when you arrived, or were you just an enormous inconvenience? Perhaps the requirement for an heir meant that grandparents were planning for your arrival long before even the birth of their own children! People yearning for grandchildren sometimes put enormous pressure on their children to have children. Even here, though, we are still way past the beginning I am thinking of. We need to go as far back in time as we can go to a place that is no longer accessible to us in the usual sense.

Your Journey starts under a Tree. In many ways it is just an ordinary tree in an ordinary setting—a Garden. It is bearing fruit, and you are looking up at the fruit through the eyes of your greatest possible grandparents. It is here in this place and this time that your Journey begins with a choice. This choice has echoed through the corridors of time ever since and affects everything you say, everything you are and everything you do. The choice is to do with ownership. Not the ownership of the fruit on this Tree, but the ownership of yourself. The choice that was made that day was a choice of independence—I can do it on my own, I don't need an owner.

A man called Adam and a woman called Eve decided that day that they wanted to be owners of their own destiny—to be filled with knowledge and wisdom that would make them independent of God—and they sealed your fate as much as their own. Because of their choice, you are faced with a life of independence because they were cast out into the world you now live in. It's no point blaming God for kicking them out of the Garden. What they did made the Garden unable to contain them any longer. This wasn't because the Garden had changed, but because *they* had changed. So now, you and I and the whole of the rest of the human race begin our Journeys standing outside of that Garden and looking in.

Now, all of the other 'beginnings' I have mentioned begin to fall into place. Why do people allow a child to suffer the agonies of being discarded at birth, raised by the kindness or otherwise of strangers, never knowing where they had come from? Why does a man force himself on a woman not caring about the consequences to her body or her soul, not to mention the creation of a child? Why do people put their own needs and desires before others and put pressure on wives and children and even grandchildren to produce an heir for them? Independence. They believe that they possess their own destinies and that is what matters. Other people become secondary considerations. Consequences become irrelevant. Life becomes a parade that everyone else dances for them.

You cannot divorce yourself from what happened under that Tree no matter how you might wish to. It so deeply affected the human race that everyone is now born with that independence stamped on their very being, as if they have a birthmark that says "I belong to me!" This goes way beyond the argument of 'nature vs. nurture'. This is a virus that has invaded every part of you. No surgical process could remove it because it is now a fundamental part of you that nothing short of death itself can remove.

So you start your Journey living in independence, learning to survive in a world you don't really belong in because you were meant to be in that Garden. There is a word we use to label that independence, and that word is sin. It is a bit unfortunate that the word is similar to another word spelled the same way, which is the thing we do when we commit an act of independent rebellion against God. I say unfortunate, because if we never committed a single act of sin, we'd still be saddled with being outside of the Garden. However it is of no consequence really, because the independent life we are forced to lead yields itself all too readily to acts of sin and we are left then with guilt, blame and shame.

I've painted a pretty gloomy picture of the start of our Journey, and you are probably wondering why I even bother to get up in the morning, but there are a lot of bright sides to all of this. For a start, if your parents didn't plan you, that is no reflection on you. You don't need to believe that it is because you are worthless! They were just stuck in this independent lifestyle being subject to their own battles with the world, thinking of themselves first before you. That does not define your worth. Being independent means that you are able to find your own worth and base it on something besides other people's choices or other people's opinions of you.

Even if you had the best parents the world has ever known, you still have the right to choose to base your worth on something other than their opinion of you. Linking your value to positive parenting is no better than linking it to bad parenting. You simply become a lucky accident that happened to draw the long straw in life. It still leaves you with no option to choose your own destiny; you are just stuck with what you have.

The amazing thing is that even though you are unique, because no-one quite looks like you, or talks like you, or thinks like you, you are not special. That's because everyone else is also unique. We all started out under that Tree and we all have to live outside the Garden. We all have to make choices, and we've all made choices that have not served us well in life's Journey. We've also made choices that have worked out very nicely, thank you. No matter how good or bad your life is or seems to be, you are just like the rest of us.

"How does that help me?" you ask. Quite simply that whatever you have gone through, someone else has also gone through it and there is a solution to your problem. I'm not up to solutions yet, but just knowing that things could get better is enough to keep you on your Journey. There is hope on the path ahead, so it is worth carrying on. Knowing that you are not the one special case that can't be helped stops you from being able to sulk your way into oblivion. It's time to get up and move on.

From the Tree you begin your Journey and it starts with a shameful walk, escorted as it were from the premises by armed guards. I'm sure some of you have experienced something like this when being made redundant or just plain fired at work. I have been asked to leave the building where I was working and collect my stuff the next day—and it's not always that pleasant. Once you are outside the Garden, there is no place else to go but outwards. There is no point standing and staring at the unattainable—there is a world to explore. But this is the last time you will be in a place where there is no turning back.

Ever after this there will always be the opportunity to return to where you were, but if you ever do, you will find that things have changed. Things used to be better in the 'good old days' so you long for a return to familiar territory, but when you get there, you find things aren't quite what they were. People change, memories play tricks on us, expectations and reality clash, and we end up dissatisfied. Life is designed to be lived by playing forward and that is always the best direction to go.

So now we come back to the circumstances of your birth. Were you planned or unplanned? Loved or hated? Born with a silver spoon in your mouth or born on the wrong side of the tracks? Who cares? You're here, and that's what matters. I for one am glad that you've come along on this Journey, and more people than you think are gladder than I am. You are not a mistake or a bottle of wine or a 'product of rape'. You are a member of the human race and you have every right not only to be here, but to elbow your way up to the front if you want to be there! Stop playing the blame game regarding your beginnings and get ready for your Journey.

Before we go on, though, you should check that you have everything you need for travelling. Every Journey begins with preparation. On a hike you need water, food, possibly maps and a compass, sensible clothing and footwear and travelling companions. When you go for a drive you need fuel. On a flight you need a passport or at least a boarding pass. On this Journey there are a number of things that will help if you pack them for travelling.

Firstly it helps to have a sense of adventure. I was driving in the Australian bush one day, trying to find a shortcut that would save me quite a few miles of driving. It was a very winding forest road with no road markings, lots of forks and intersections and a very rough surface. I eventually found my way back to the main road, but for a long time when my wife would ask me where my spirit of adventure was, I'd tell her that I'd lost it on that forest road! If you've lost your spirit of adventure, then come along anyway, but if not, get prepared to find some places you've never been before.

Bring along a good supply of expectancy. We get what we expect out of life, and if we don't expect much we won't be disappointed. That may be a safe way to live life, but it's a very sad one. If you've learned to stop expecting, you are in very abundant company, but if you can lay hold of any, expectancy is a good travelling companion.

Pack your bag full of questions. I'm not qualified to give you answers, but questions are an excellent way to get the most out of a Journey. "What's over the next hill?" is a question that will get you to the top of that hill. "I wonder what water from a mountain stream tastes like?" will get you a delightful drinking experience that is worth getting your shoes wet for. And "What have I been missing out on in my life?" is the way to experience almost anything that you can imagine.

Most importantly don't forget your emotions. Be prepared to laugh, to cry, to sing, to get angry, to love and even to hate because some things need to be hated. Life is to be experienced at an emotional level, not processed like a computer manipulating a stream of data. Smell the roses, chase the butterflies, jump in puddles and make snow angels. Make the most of everything you feel because every one of those feelings screams out "I'm alive!" This Journey is most definitely to be enjoyed.

So, if you have your bag packed, we're ready to get started.

Discovery

MAGINE LOOKING AT LIFE AGAIN through completely fresh eyes as you did when you first came into this world. Very seldom do people's memories extend back into early childhood, notwithstanding attempts by some to access those memories using various dubious methods. But when you are so young, everything is new. You have no idea what a face is, what light is, what hot or cold is or what food is. But you are about to find out.

As soon as you have the dexterity to do so, you put everything into your mouth. Taste is one of the first ways you have of actually experiencing life for yourself. Hearing things, seeing things, smelling things and even touching things are a bit remote in some ways. Taste is a way of really getting up close and personal with something. The response to taste is one of the most evocative experiences we can have. It not only encompasses flavour; it tells us about texture, hardness and usefulness. At least at this tender young age, whether it is edible or not is the most important indicator of how useful it is! If it's not edible it probably isn't worth anything so you throw it away, but not before coating in a good deal of slobber.

There is a verse in the Bible that says "Taste and see that the Lord is good". Taste is an excellent metaphor for experiencing someone (in this case, God) or something in such a way that will enable you to make a judgement about whether it is good. We learned that from eating the fruit of that Tree. Somewhere along the line we tend to lose that. We substitute taste for two things, observation and opinion.

Observation is the process of placing a glass box around something so that we can look at it but not have to get involved with it. We substitute viewing for visiting and so we watch travel programs, cooking shows and DIY segments on television. TV is a great way to miss out on a great deal of life. It lulls you into the false sense of having been there and done that without getting up from your sofa. You think "I should go to Greece" then reach for the remote to watch car bombs going off in Tel Aviv. The world becomes something that happens to other people.

All you have to do is look at the ratio of people in the stands of a football stadium to the people on the pitch to realise how few people truly experience life. True, those who go to football games do so to "experience the atmosphere", but the ones truly living the game are the ones sweating and bleeding down there on the field of play. Participating is something that 'somebody else' does because the effort of getting ourselves to the point where we could actively engage is just too much. We experience the game vicariously through our sports heroes, but we don't get our own hands dirty.

Opinion, on the other hand, is the means of avoiding having to experience something personally because somebody has already told us what it is like. Whether the report is good or bad, we can push that experience off to the future because we already know, at least as much as we want to know. By stacking up opinions we can protect ourselves from most of life and just stick to the safe confines of our little corner of the universe. Get enough of them and you know virtually everything! Get even a few of them and you have an excuse to stop trying.

Opinions fall into two kinds—those we agree with and those we don't. It doesn't matter what kind we subscribe to—someone else has done the research so we don't have to. The problem is that we never truly own these opinions. We pull whichever ones we need out of our bag and use them to justify our behaviour. Even two opposing opinions can be trotted out right after one another to distance ourselves from something we don't want to be bothered with.

When you are a baby, however, things are different. The universe just isn't big enough. You look for open spaces, open doors, things to climb up on or things to climb down into. People of my age are probably responsible for that terror of modern life, the childproof cap! We didn't have them in my childhood, but the youthful need to experience the delights of washing up detergent, headache tablets and toilet cleaner made some bright spark feel the need to ensure the preservation of the species. An unnecessary contribution in my opinion, but if you've experienced a child being saved by one, I'll keep my opinions to myself.

This search for space leads us to discover something that will affect us for the rest of our lives: boundaries. Sooner or later we run up against something that just won't give. Maybe it's the front door. Perhaps it is a baby gate stopping us from getting into the kitchen. Whatever it is, these things make us realise that life has limits. Even when we are old enough to go outside, there are always limits. "Don't go past that post!" "Make sure you stay in sight." "Stay away from Mr. Smith's front yard!" Of course these are all for our protection and well-being, but it doesn't take long for us to learn that life has borders.

Children's brains don't readily grasp the distinction between what we are *allowed* to do and what we are *able* to do. Soon many of us begin to believe that we are just not able to do certain things. Our parents often do their best to coach us out of that self-limiting attitude without realising that they probably put it in there in the first place! I believed I was unable to ride a bike until I was in my early twenties, until I got on one for the first time and I was a natural. I have never done the Tour de France, but two-wheeled vehicles no longer limit me.

What impact does this have on our Journey? Quite simply it means that we get off to a slow start! The desire to just stay at home is instilled into us from a very early age. Even the word 'wanderlust' implies that staying at home is a virtue and travel is a sin! This means that Journeying becomes a learned behaviour not a natural practice, even though we were born with the desire to explore. Of course I'm not trying to make the pendulum swing the other way—to make staying at home a sin and travel a virtue! Nor am I focussing on literal travel. It is just the mindset that 'home' is good and 'away from home' is risky, that excludes us from possibilities.

In this sense, 'home' is whatever is safe, and 'away from home' is the unfamiliar, unknown 'other' that you face if you stray away from 'safe'. To go back to childhood, the first time you visit Grandma's house it is strange and scary, but unless your grandmother is a complete terror, it soon becomes familiar, safe, and an extension of 'home'. I'm not advocating taking your children to scary people's houses to beat this mindset out of them! This book is not about parenting. This is about you and your Journey and why, perhaps even now, you step over the threshold of 'safe' very reluctantly.

Journeying is always about the unknown. Going is something that happens whether the place you are going to is familiar or not. In the introduction I mentioned the Confucius quote: "A Journey of a thousand miles begins with a single step". I'm not sure he would have said precisely that because he would never have heard of 'miles', but the principle is there. That single step begins with a decision, to step over the threshold of your 'known' and into the unknown. Unless you have lived in a bubble all of your life, you have already taken that step at least once.

So what happens to you when you do that? Do you think, "Oh, well, that wasn't so bad!" when the scary thing doesn't happen, or are your worst fears confirmed when something jumps out at you from behind a bush and goes "Boo!"? The answer doesn't actually matter because the Journey is still out there and it is still beckoning to you. Sure life sucks sometimes, but get over it. Life is great sometimes too! It's living it that's important. Avoiding it just allows it to slip by you at the rate of 3,600 seconds an hour and fall into the bag of regrets.

Has your life of discovery stopped, and if so, when did it stop? You've probably heard the saying that "Today is the first day of the rest of your life." When it is literally the first day of your life, everything is a discovery. Every taste is new. Every sound has to have a meaning attached to it. Everyone you meet is a stranger. What if your spouse was a complete stranger to you? You'd probably ask them things about themselves, get to know what they like, find out what they thought about you. Why assume that just because you have been living with them for a decade or more that you no longer need to find out those things?

Have your children become so familiar to you that nothing they do interests you any more? Or perhaps you show interest merely to tick the 'good parenting' box, not because you really care. If you had a foreign exchange student under your roof for the first time, you'd probably make the effort to get to know them a little. After all they are from a different culture, maybe even with a different language. In case you haven't noticed, your kids, especially if they are teenagers, *are* from a different culture with a different language and part of your Journey could be to get to know them again.

Your parents may not understand you, but there is no reason for that to be mutual. When we have children of our own, we begin to get some sympathy for our own mums and dads and we can finally put ourselves in their shoes. Discovering what makes them tick before you get that sympathy may be a way you can make life more interesting for yourself. You may find them to be quite amazing people. My own grown up son just recently said to me that he realised he had never asked me about a certain part of my life and wanted to know about it.

Even discovering strangers can yield enormous treasures. Don't forget that all of your friends were complete strangers to you at one time. That makes every stranger a potential friend. Of course your mother told you to never talk to strangers, but you are not a child any more! There are times and places to avoid strangers, but there are many, many more times and places, where getting to know them is a perfectly healthy exercise. Being afraid of every stranger we meet is decidedly unhealthy.

Has your Journey of discovery excluded God? Perhaps you have decided that there is no God to discover, or that He has no relevance to you. Perhaps you know Him very well. In any case, go back to your first day when you were open to finding out whatever you could about Him. Go back beyond all the reasons and arguments for counting Him out of the game. Then open yourself up to the possibility that something you have experienced may have soured you to the idea of the presence of God in your life. Quite often it is that sort of reason rather than any logic or pragmatism that is the real cause of atheism.

So let's put you back on your hands and knees again. You've bumped your head on the baby gate, been told to stay away from the TV remote, had the cat's biscuits removed from your tiny fingers, so you crawl back into the lounge and sulk for a bit. But it's not too long before your ache to discover new things gets you into trouble again. You keep doing this until you learn all of the boundaries you aren't allowed to cross. Your world becomes defined and packaged and you know your place in it.

After a while you learn to walk, and the bumping and telling off starts all over again at a higher pace. You also learn to talk and begin to communicate with the big people in your life. And you become self aware, and at some stage, usually around two years old, you begin to challenge the defined and bounded world you have been made to live in. Then begins a wonderful time that some parents refer to as 'the terrible twos'.

During the so-called terrible twos, you begin challenging everything, and the worst thing that can happen to you at that time is that the adults in your life give in to your boundary pushing and let you do anything you want. The second worst thing is to make your boundaries so restrictive that they choke the life out of you and make you just give up. This is also the time when you will learn respect, or lack of it, for those adults. By the time you have reached three years old or more and everyone has started to lick their wounds, you are a dramatically different person.

You are now saddled with something that will give you a lot of service for the rest of your life. It is a simple statement that you will trot out many times as an excuse for anything you don't want to do. "That's just who I am". After all, you've earned it! You've just spent a year or more throwing everything you can at the boundaries and limits and found out what you can move and what you can't move. You know who you are and it has become hard to persuade you otherwise.

Of course this process is far from finished, but a remarkable amount of your 'programming' is now complete. This is not necessarily all bad. You need structure and order to help you survive life. Remember the Tree. You are independent. You have to survive. So you arm yourself with hundreds or even thousands of little coping strategies that help you to live in a hostile world. These can be all kinds of things. "Daddy didn't give me a toy when I asked him, so I must be bad." You don't want to be bad, but knowing that you are bad helps you cope with not having your requests granted. Disappointment is then avoided, as is hurt. When you don't get what you want, that's OK because that's the way the world is supposed to be.

"Mummy never spends any time with me so I must not be worth spending time with." This makes relationships so much easier to handle! Rejection is a perfectly normal part of life. It also works in the positive too. "I get attention when I'm clever so I'll cultivate being clever then people will like me". The end result of this is that we make a decision as to whether we are good or bad. This decision will affect you for the rest of your life. It's not set in stone yet, and a good teacher, good friend or helpful relative can still assist you to change your decision about being 'bad' and equally a bad teacher, bad friend or unhelpful relative may turn you to the dark side so to speak. But by and large, barring some form of intervention, before you are even old enough to really evaluate the consequences of it, you have mostly become the person you will retreat to when things get hard.

Then suddenly one day you are faced with something completely unfamiliar. It is an open door, not just to another room, but to the outside world. And from there your Journey takes a very different course.

Paths

O F COURSE YOU HAVE SEEN the outside world before. I'm not talking about this as if you'd been kept isolated for two to three years then suddenly formally introduced to the world. But there comes a time when you are aware that there is a big world out there waiting for your discovery. You get taken to a playground and are allowed to find swings, slides, sandpits and seats (that your parents sit on!). If the playground is fenced you'll be left to explore pretty much all of it, but if it's not you'll soon find yourself getting told 'Don't go over there, it's not safe'.

That's OK, you are used to this. You weren't allowed into the kitchen or the laundry room. There were some things you couldn't touch. But when you are walking to and from the playground, or round a park, or in a forest, you find a new taboo that maybe you haven't heard before. 'Stay on the path, you might get lost.'

In your house there are no paths. There are rooms and doors. But out in the world there are paths everywhere! You soon find that your place is on the footpath, and cars make it unsafe to go on the road. There are paths through the supermarket car park. There are paths in parks, in the country, in the city. Pretty much everywhere we go we are being directed to go certain ways. Vast tracts of grass go unexplored because we have to 'stay on the path'.

Some of us never find out what the terrible consequences of violating this universal commandment are. What monsters lay waiting for us to get lost on the grass or in the forest if we stray? These days the monsters sometimes have hairless skin, walk upright on two legs and hold down jobs in the City. But sometimes the taboo is just about keeping the grass beautiful. We just don't know because we just don't stray.

As a young child I once spotted a sign that must have said something like 'Trespassers will be Prosecuted' and in my mind, that memory is associated with a 'Keep off the Grass' sign. I asked my mother what 'Persecuted' meant. I had picked the wrong word and she answered for the word I actually used, not questioning where I'd got it from. So she said that it meant to be killed! Imagine my fear of breaking the grass taboos then! No matter what she said or meant or what I said, heard or understood, it helps explain my obsession with staying on paths even now.

Of course some of you never stayed on the paths, despite constant nagging from your mother, so you have no idea what I am talking about. To you the path is a constraint not needing to be held to. Some of you don't even notice the paths. So, you step over flowerbeds, jump fences, run across the grass with joyful abandon, and never encounter the monsters. You will get there before I do because I will be on the longer route. Or you'll arrive after me because you are distracted by something beautiful while I am obsessed with getting 'there'.

Then there are those paths that lead to places we are just told we should not go. Paths bearing signs like "Danger: Hazardous Chemicals", "Authorised Personnel Only", or ways simply barred by a pass code, or an armed or unarmed guard. As very young children we don't understand those words but we can learn to recognise the places that we really must not go and in those cases there are no unknown monsters or threats of what might happen, just a clear intention that we are not to go there.

Through all of this we learn about the structure of the world in terms of a network of interconnecting paths. I need a path to get from here to there. Or I need to bypass the paths to get from here to there. The paths are never irrelevant. They are either a guide or a challenge! They are a vehicle for access to something, either by following them to their destination or leaving them to explore the unknown. Neither approach is right or wrong. I am not talking about moral paths here—just things that have been made.

There is a poem that illustrates the nature of paths perfectly. It is called *The Calf Path*.

The Calf Path

One day through the primeval wood
A calf walked home as good calves should;
But made a trail all bent askew,
A crooked path as all calves do . . .
The trail was taken up the very next day
By a lame dog that passed that way;
And then a wise bell weather sheep
Pursued that trail o'er hill and steep,
And drew the flock behind him, too
As good Bell Weather always do,
And from that day, o'er hill and glade
Through these old weeds a path was made . . .
And many men wound in and out,
And dodged and turned and bent about
And uttered words of righteous wrath
Because "twas such a crooked path . . ."
The forest path became a lane
That bent and turned and turned again;
The crooked lane became a road,
Where many a poor horse with his load
Toiled on beneath the burning sun
And traveled some three miles in one . . .
The years past on it swiftness fleet,
The road became a village street;
And this before men were aware,

A city's crowded thoroughfare . . .
Each day a hundred thousand bout
Followed this zigzagging calf about,
And o'er his crooked journey went
The traffic of a continent.
A hundred thousand men were led
By one calf near three centuries dead.
They followed still his croaked way,
And last one hundred year a day;
For this such reverence was lent
To a well-established precedent.
For men are prone to go it blind
Along the calf path of the mind,
And work away from sun to sun
To do what other men have done.
They follow in the beaten track
And in and out, and forth and back,
And still their devious course pursue
To keep the path that others do.
They keep the path a sacred groove
Along which all their lives they move;
But how the wise old wood gods laugh
Who saw the first primeval calf!

—Sam Walter Foss

There are paths that we can see and either walk on or escape from, but there are also paths that we can't see but we are also expected to stay on them. Here's one example. I grow up, go to school, high school, college, university, get a job, get married, work until I'm 65 then retire and die. Here's another one. I grow up and go to school but I get married before university, have children and be a mother then a grandmother until I die. That last one would be hard for me as a man, but I'm sure some of you recognise it. And of course I chose those two because they are very traditional and often followed for reasons that are long forgotten.

Just like the calf path, many of the predefined paths through life exist for arbitrary reasons, not for any practical purpose! If you are of a nature that inclines you to follow paths, then you'll follow paths through life too. If you consider paths to be mere suggestions then you'll probably be dimly aware that expectations were put on you as a child, but you didn't let them hold you back. You'll go through life in a less directed fashion and see and do things that many of us only see on TV.

The worst of both worlds, however, is to be inclined to follow those paths through life, but failing to do so for whatever reason. For example in the first 'path' above, failing to get a university degree, or in the second 'path', failing to find a husband. One failure often leads to another and we make the conclusion that WE are the cause. If I fail, then that defines me as a failure and so I settle down into a lifetime of failure because that's all I'm worth. All the while being unaware that the very expectations that create what we call a 'failure', result from following a 'path' that we weren't necessarily bound to in the first place!

It is virtually as bad a situation for me to be a path dodger and find myself, due to circumstances, being herded down one of those paths and end up being trapped in a situation that is not what I had planned! The feeling of being a defeated loser is just as real in that place as it is in the other. No matter how successful you are, if you aren't doing what you always wanted to do, you will be dissatisfied. You are stuck on a back alley somewhere along the calf path.

The really great thing to notice about paths, though, is that they join on to other paths. Have you ever walked along a forest path, especially as a child, and found another path crossing? Do you remember that burning curiosity as you looked down it? Can you recall the delight as you get to walk along it or the deep disappointment as you are led along the original path?

Of course on a forest trail you never know what it might lead you to, especially if it is unsigned. Having done a fair bit of walking in England, I can tell you that it isn't much of a problem because you won't have to walk far before finding a road, farmhouse or village. But walking on forest paths in Australia is a different matter! You could easily get lost for days. It's the same with life's paths. When you find an adjoining path and you look along it wondering if you should go that way, you might get lost! But you may also find your dream. It all depends on how you look at it.

Paths also go through things and beside things, but some people are so focussed on the path or the destination that they forget to look at what is around them. Have you ever driven somewhere and realised that you have no idea how you got there? You got so lost in thought that you drove completely on autopilot. If you look back at your life you'll find much the same. At the time of writing I am 54 years old, but can I access 54 years worth of memories? What have I been doing since December 1956? I honestly only have highlights.

Take the time to look at things along the way. As the hackneyed cliché goes, take time to smell the roses; because hackneyed or not, clichéd or not, it's valid! We miss the most important things in life sometimes because of the most trivial things. I looked at my grandkids in church the other week and I realised that I am only going to see them at that age once! Next week they'll be a week older. I could miss an important part of their lives because I chose to do something unimportant like straighten up a chair or pick up a piece of rubbish instead of going over and spending some time with them.

Illumination is very important to paths, especially at night. In some parts of the world you can walk along a dark path in the dead of night with no fear, but there are places where you would do that only if you had a death wish. The lights are there to show you where you are but they are also there to discourage unsavoury people from attacking you. Generally speaking, evil hates the light and stays away from it. Walking along a lighted path is usually (though not always) safer than walking on a dark path.

Often in our lives we are faced up with dark paths. Many stray along them and then someone either takes advantage of them or even abuses them, but also sometimes we ourselves are corrupted by the darkness along the path and join in with those that take advantage of or abuse others. A dark path does not start with a grand entrance and a sign that says "Abandon hope all ye who enter here!" It starts with a temptation, or a thought that perhaps a little deviation from the straight and narrow never hurt anyone. People who are path avoiders can find this easier to understand than those rigidly addicted to paths, however someone who always stays on a path may doggedly follow a dark path if they get lured on to one.

There is another sort of dark path that we travel from time to time. The 23rd Psalm in the Bible says "Though I walk through the valley of the shadow of death, I will fear no evil." There are times in our lives that the paths become dark because of grief and sorrow or due to circumstances that try to tear us down and destroy us. The sad thing is that many people who find themselves along that path stay there. In the case of grief this may be due to a fear that leaving that place will dishonour the memory of the departed loved one, or fear of losing the last remaining connection to the person. In the case of personal hardship, however, it is often because of a belief that somehow we deserved the terrible thing to happen to us and we need to stay there.

The good news is that the valley of the shadow of death is something we can walk *through*. We don't need to settle there. Grief is a hard place to be in, but there is a way out. At its keenest, we can believe that the pain will never go away and we'll never love anyone again. If we will allow ourselves to grieve in a healthy fashion we can put the grief into its place and then move on with our lives. I will come back to this point in a later chapter.

You might be saying at this point "Isn't this book about a Journey? Aren't we all on paths?" That depends on your attitude to paths. I am still on my Journey if I am laying on the grass in the park, sitting in a boat in the middle of a mountain lake, leaping from the top of a pole in a forest or running a half marathon. I can leave the paths. I like paths, but they can be my enemies as much as my friends. I have been on calf paths and dark paths and been stuck in dead ends. But beside every path, is a way off the path.

Sure, sometimes that way is a vertical climb, or a 2,000 foot drop or rapids or even toxic waste! In that case to choose to stay on the path is a very wise one. But when the side of the path is an open forest or a grassy field or a fordable stream, why not go there? Think about it for a minute. Why not? What is it that keeps you where you are, doing what you do day in, day out, nothing ever changing? Is your dream on the path? More than likely it is not. It is risky to leave paths, but without risk there is no gain. You'll just keep doing what you've always done.

Now we need to take a look around us for something different. If you look closely you'll find something you've missed until now. You are not alone on the path. You have friends.

Friends

* * * * * * * * * * * * * *

YOU MAY HAVE READ THE last paragraph of the previous chapter and decided that no-one is on the path with you. Well even if there's been no-one up until now, there is me. I am gathering that since you've managed to read this far you must be enjoying the Journey, so I must be at the very least a tolerable travelling companion. So if you are prepared to bear with me for a while, I'll address your situation later in the chapter. For now I want to talk to those of you who do have travelling companions.

I am going to go with the most general definition of friends that I can think of. A friend is someone with whom you are on reasonable speaking terms. You don't have to be blood brothers to be friends for this part of the Journey. I would even dare to suggest that even your enemies are your friends. Someone who is your enemy won't sugar coat their opinion of you, so you usually know where you stand. In any case, an enemy's opinion of you isn't about you, it's about them. In that respect you have a lot in common with them.

But more on that later. For now we'll stick with positive relationships. If you have brothers and sisters you may or may not have been friends with them. I remember being friends with my brother most of the time but picking on my little sister (I hasten to add that I am her friend now!). Then there were cousins who I came in contact with, or the 'sort-of' cousins who were just children of friends of the family. You can form kinds of 'de facto' friendships with them. But then there are the friends that you actually find for yourself, usually starting at school. These are the ones that you encounter in the crowds and that somehow you manage to get on with so well that you'll seek them out.

I think you probably get the difference I'm talking about. You can get on with a relative or a friend of the family OK, but you won't actually seek them out or go out of your way to contact them. A friend is someone that you asked mum, "Can I go over to so-and-so's house to play after school?" A friend is someone you wrote notes to. A friend is someone who seeks you out as well as you seeking them out.

Who knows how these attachments form? You strike up a conversation, notice something in common, find that you can get on, start to spend time together and soon it becomes a habit. You find yourself wanting their company, and being better off, or at least feeling better, for having engaged in that company. The true test of such attachments is how they survive after the first time you find something you disagree on.

Make no mistake; no friendship is immune from that crisis point. There are the points where you like something that he hasn't heard of and the discovery leads to him appreciating something new. Or when you like dogs and she likes cats and you just agree to disagree. I am talking about the time when you discover that he likes The Rolling Stones and you passionately hate rock music of any kind. Or when you share your love for modern art and she insists that such art is mindless rubbish that only a fool could appreciate.

That's the point at which you have your first 'lover's tiff'. Oh, don't worry; I haven't swapped from friendship to dating here. But the same sort of breakdown that characterises the romantic relationship's so-called 'lover's quarrels' appears here also. The 'honeymoon' phase of the friendship is over; now you have to find a way of moving it forward despite the difference just discovered. Or abandon it—some friendships just don't make it past this point. You both have to weigh up the prices and benefits of continuing and make a mutual decision to put the difference aside, or put one another aside.

This is where you learn an important lesson in forgiveness. Your mother made you 'say sorry' to and 'forgive' your siblings and cousins, but with a friend, you have to make the choice to truly forgive from your heart, or it's over. There is no policeman here; it's just you, your conscience and your friend, unless God is a part of your life. The thing is that some of the best, most long lasting and precious friendships have to go through this process often. If you think that this phase of a relationship is bad and to be avoided, then you have probably only ever had superficial relationships.

The true power of any friendship comes from its ability to face the refining power of a major argument and to come forth stronger than before. Steel is strongest when it has been refined and beaten, the more times the better. The more superficial the refinement process used on steel, the more brittle and breakable it is. The famous Japanese Samurai swords are made by a process of folding and hammering that increases the strength of the blade. Friendship works like that. By encountering a rift and forging ourselves back together to work it out again and again, we become bonded together inseparably.

Relationships come in three main flavours. Firstly there is the kind that is all give on your side and all take on the other. Your friend is always a 'friend in need'. They have the problems and you have the answers. Or if you don't, it doesn't matter really; they always expect you to support them. Don't even bother trying to share a trying time with this kind of friend, they'll just turn it around and make it all about them. This isn't a bad thing—we all need somebody to lean on, as the song says, but if we don't have anyone leaning on us we never get to give without expectation of return.

The second flavour is the type of relationship where you are the needy one and there's someone to whom you always go to get support. Never mind what they are going through, this is about me! Can't you see I'm hurting? If you have this kind of friend you probably always feel better after time spent with them, but spare a thought for the stuff they may be going through. Because very often they wouldn't dream of burdening you with their woes! They can only see your pain and theirs takes a back seat. Even for the most generous soul that wears thin after a while.

The third flavour is much rarer. That's the kind that has a more or less equal level of support on both sides. You're both prepared to bear one another's burdens—you listen to one another attentively, give support when needed, accept it when you need it and remain considerate of one another's needs. Lasting marriages are built around this kind of friendship.

There are also infinite variations between those three types, but those are the basic three. None of them is right or wrong, but if you have all draining relationships and no uplifting ones, you will wear yourself out. And if you have all supportive relationships and no demanding ones, you will never grow; you will always be a big fat baby.

Make no mistake, though, no matter how altruistic you think you are, a friendship is never about the other person—it's always about you. No matter how supportive you are, you are acting out a need inside you to be that supporter. Your need to be needed is sufficiently strong to seek out someone who needs you. No matter how different the person with whom you are friends with may seem to be, there will be a reflection of you in there and it is that reflection of you that you are subconsciously seeking out. If your friend is challenging you, then you are growing, so it is about you. If it is about companionship, it is about you.

Does that mean that there are no altruistic friendships? I won't purport to be an expert on every relationship on the planet to say that none of them is altruistic, but certainly there is one that is. Not all of you will relate to this, but your Creator is in an unendingly altruistic relationship with you. God is a friend who gives unceasingly and takes nothing. Some of you agree with me wholeheartedly. Some of you think I'm nuts. Some of you think I don't know what I'm talking about. That's OK. But from my point of view my friendship with God is all give on His part and mostly take on mine. And He asks nothing in return for that. Of course we worship Him, and give Him praise, but He will do anything for us even if we show no gratitude at all.

What about you friendless people whom I invited to come on the Journey with me at the beginning of the chapter? Perhaps some of you have realised as you have read thus far that maybe you had friends and didn't know it. If so, then hopefully I have done you a service. But some of you are still standing alone on life's path, defying me to carry on and give them some hope! So look around you. You have no-one on the path with you. No companions, no enemies, not even a God! So what about yourself?

What is your relationship to yourself? Now is not the time to run and hide! Don't tell me that you don't talk to yourself. What do you say? Science tells us that we speak around 1500 words a minute to ourselves in what is called 'self talk', most of it at a subconscious level. Much of it tends to be negative. Very often, the type of friend we are to ourselves directly affects the type of relationships, or the lack of relationships that we have with others. We are the one friend that we have that we can't run away from. We are the one we are most likely to offend and the least likely to forgive. Until we learn how to live with ourselves we won't learn how to live with others.

That of course leads me to the way that our relationship to ourselves affects our relationship to others in a twist that will probably surprise you. What is it that most irritates you about other people? Look closely at those things. It will probably startle you to think that what you see in others is nothing to do with them. It is all about you. Some of you probably already thought it was always about you anyway, but seriously, when something somebody does really rubs you up the wrong way, what you are seeing is your mirror. If you will honestly look at what it is in you that reflects that behaviour, you will see that you are guilty of the same fault, or at some level, you are doing the same thing, even if it is in a different area.

I had an experience recently of being annoyed at a sales person. I believe in the principle I have just described so I asked myself, what is it in me that is reflected in what annoys me about this sales person? Remember it is not about them. What is annoying me is nothing to do with what they have done. It is always about something in me. They may not even be doing what I perceive them to be doing! I am seeing an image; something that ticks me off. When I honestly looked, I realised that I am sometimes very pushy with my wife. I tell her what to do instead of gently suggesting what might serve her and help her. What I was perceiving in this other person, is something I am very guilty of in my own relationships.

So now we come to enemies. It is said that your enemy's enemy is your friend, but as I have already suggested, I believe that your enemy *is* your friend. Think about it. Someone who doesn't like you will probably not try to gloss over their opinion of you! If anything, given the chance, they will be brutally honest. If you want to know what you are truly like, ask an enemy. They may not tell you anything nice, but they certainly won't tell you that you are wonderful and that you are just fine the way you are! If you realise that what they dislike about you is a reflection of something in them, then you are free to let them hold that opinion because it has nothing to do with you. You might also learn something useful about the way you are presenting yourself that will help you to change.

Unless you live in a complete vacuum you are surrounded by friends. There are people you haven't even met yet that are your friends—they just haven't gotten to know you yet. Try saying hello to a few people. Think about the ones you already call 'friend'. What are they reflecting back to you? What are you reflecting back to them? Think about the ones you call 'enemies'. How did they become enemies? Are you modelling something in life that is repelling them when you could be reconciled to them by changing something in you?

And think about why it is that you think you have no friends. What are you exhibiting that makes you unappealing? Be honest with yourself. You may as well; you have no-one else who will be honest with you yet. If you are truly serious about having friends, be prepared to pay the price it takes to change you, because you can't change anyone else.

One of the things we all do with friends when we are younger is to play games. You even play games with yourself. So let's take time in our Journey to look at a few.

Games

* * * * * * * * * * * * * *

KIDS LIKE GAMES. SOME ADULTS don't like them, but that's because they learn to dislike them. Generally speaking you don't have to teach children to like games—they do so instinctively. Probably one of the earliest games you got to play was Hide and Seek. You learned simple rules to a simple game.

For the seeker:—

1. No peeking
2. Count to 100 (or 10 or 3!)
3. When you've done counting call out that you're coming
4. Find the other person

For the hider:—

5. Hide properly
6. Don't make any noise
7. Don't give away the position of any other hiders

There had to be players. Solitaire or Patience only requires you as a player but most games, especially those you played as a child, require at least one other player. Parents will be all too familiar with the cries of 'Can you play so-and-so with me? Johnny won't play.' It can be a great blow to your self esteem when no-one wants to play with you, or they choose you last because you are the only one left. Here is another fertile breeding ground for childhood coping strategies that stay with us long into adulthood.

Then there is the 'field of play'. For a board game it is the playing board. When you were very young, you probably had a lot of difficulty with that concept! The playing pieces, be they tokens, dice or little figurines tend to wander all around the room when small children are involved. Larger fields of play are involved with games like Hide and Seek. That one probably got changed when your mother yelled at you to stay out of her wardrobe while hiding. Staying within the field of play can be a source of frustration; for the player who doesn't want to and for the other players, annoyed by the player who doesn't want to!

You also learned other things about being a sore loser or a gracious winner. You learned that people cheat, and that playing fair cuts both ways. Games model life. What you learn in the playground carries on out into the marketplace. Failure to learn the lessons that games teach us leads to failure in life. And you thought games were trivial and unimportant!

Typically games are broken into two main kinds, games of chance, games of skill and then into combinations of those two kinds. Now I am of the opinion that chance is a misleading concept. If I roll a dice people say that the outcome is chance, but the truth of the matter is that the force I use in the roll, the angle it leaves my hand, the angle it hits the table top, all contribute mathematically and physically to a predictable outcome if we just knew how to do the maths. The practical outcome however is that we don't know how to do the maths, so it comes out, on average, to a 16.7% chance of any one number turning up on a standard 6-sided die.

A game like Snakes and Ladders is all chance. You just roll the die, count off the numbers, and go where the board tells you to go. A game like Monopoly has some skill involved because as well as the statistically random dice throws there are decisions to be made about how to buy, sell and develop property. Your skill in operating those aspects of the game affects the outcome. Then there are games like chess that have no chance element at all. Chess, in particular, is all skill.

But I would like to introduce another word into this discussion: choice. I put it to you that there are really only games of chance and games of choice. Snakes and Ladders has no choices past whether to play or not. It is a purely 'victim' game. You are the victim of the throws of the die, the snakes and even the ladders. When I am playing the game with little children (when I get collared and don't know a way to avoid it!) I don't like it when I get a huge ladder that puts me way ahead and makes me look like the big mean grown up. I have no control over the outcome of the game; I am just a victim to it.

Monopoly has a lot of choices but I am still a victim to the dice throws, the properties I land on and the cards that turn up. I can make all the right choices about property but still get aced by a bad run of dice throws that drains my cash. But whatever happens I still have choices about how I play. I can suck the fun right out of the game for everyone else by being a poor sport. It is a game that has opportunities for me to show kindness and generosity, but most people who like to play it also like to play it hard and mean.

Chess on the other hand is all about choices. From the first move, whether you play it as a novice and just randomly pick a piece to move, or as a more seasoned player who picks an opening gambit, you exercise choice. Barring a force of nature tipping the board over, it will continue to depend on the choices of both players until the conclusion. Yes there is skill involved in the choices, but the most important skill is making the right choices.

Now please don't try to tell me that life isn't a game! A lot of people will tell me that life is far too serious to just dismiss as being a game. Life and death issues are at stake. But that is an illusion. Just because the stakes are higher, doesn't mean it isn't a game. Think about it. There are players, rules and a field of play, just like a board game. It is a game with elements of both choice and chance. You can be a good sport or a bad sport (although the possibility of extremes is infinite), a sore loser or a good loser, a generous winner or a stingy winner.

Just because the game of life has severe consequences does not make it any less a game. If you break the rules you can lose money, lose happiness, lose you freedom or even lose your life. You can also get rich, have a type of happiness, stay free and stay alive. Don't get me wrong—there are long term prices to breaking the rules that may not be reflected in the short term results, but cheating often seems to pay off in life.

Also if you stick to the rules you can have all the same things happen. Playing by the rules is no guarantee that everything will go your way. Sometimes people will simply resent that you are a 'goody two shoes' and take it out on you. Or they will see that you are content to stay within the rules without challenging anything and just bypass you. Sometimes rule breakers just get the right kind of attention.

Is the game of life, then, a game of choice or a game of chance? There is a deep and important question to be answered here! Many people live life as though it were a game of chance—they just wait and wait for their lucky number to come up and let everything happen to them. Nothing is their fault—it's the government or the economy or the weather, never them. That's fine—if that's you, how is that working for you? That is the lottery mentality. You buy a ticket along with a million other people and convince yourself that that gives you an even chance of getting rich on Saturday evening!

There are also people who live it as a game of choice in which it all depends on them. You have self made men and self made women who stride through life as colossi, sweeping all before them until they get struck down by financial disaster, broken relationships, sickness or death. What if life were a balance of choices and chances that enable us to go through life making the best of what is dished up to us, but keeps us humble enough that we do have to depend on others and perhaps even on God?

At least then, the game is interesting. There are winners and losers, but if the winners and the losers helped both themselves and others, it could also be rewarding.

So coming back to our Journey, as you began to play games and began to interact with other people and with life in the game context, suddenly you discovered a new phrase to help you through life. Johnny pulled your hair or Susie spilled your drink and you somehow got in trouble. That's when it came out at top volume: "IT'S NOT FAIR!" Games give us a first hand experience with something called fairness.

What is fairness? It is the idea that if something good happens to you it should happen to me as well. Or if something bad happens to me but it was your fault, you should carry the burden of the consequences. It takes us a long time to learn that life isn't fair and that fairness is neither promised nor guaranteed to anyone. You'd think we'd have learned that from the playground, but somehow, we cling onto the idea that life ought to be giving us a better deal.

This desire for fairness is a two-edged sword. On the one hand it is a desire that there should be some overarching good in the world that means we are not going to get targeted all the time without someone looking out for us. On the other hand it provides with an excuse for lashing out and being unfair to others. After a number of incidents in which Mum slaps you for something your brother or sister did, you start to take the law into your own hands and make up new rules to the game.

If this goes on long enough we start to develop some more coping strategies. We'll find little ways in which to steal back what we think was unjustly taken from us. We'll shut down and refuse to play the game. We'll find ways that we can be in charge of the game and make sure we don't get hurt again. And these strategies also last way beyond childhood.

If your way of coping with unfairness is to withdraw from the game, then that's how you will play life. You will be faced with a new opportunity or a new challenge in life and you'll let it pass you by. After all, life's not fair so why should you even try? If you learned to cope as a child by stealing sweets from your brother's secret stash, you'll steal stationery or time or even money as a way of compensating for perceived unfairness at work.

The reason for this is that games are life and life is a game. If games weren't as real and engaging as life we wouldn't play them. When we play Monopoly, the engagement with money and property and debt and taking advantage of others reminds us of life, where we really would like to have the kind of money that would allow us to be property tycoons or businessmen or landlords. If not literally, then at least at some level we want to experience prosperity of some kind.

Even the game I mentioned first off in the chapter, Hide and Seek, has connections to activities we will take on in later life—dating, job seeking, house hunting and even travel.

You wake up every morning and discover that it's your turn to move. You can do that by the shake of a dice. You can allow chance and circumstance to dictate what you will do for the day. You can move by making a choice to involve yourself in some kind of activity that will serve a specific purpose. You can play according to some kind of strategic pattern that will work towards a specific endgame. You can spontaneously choose moves and hope that if you do it often enough and with enough power then you are bound to hit something!

The important thing is to move. Some days it will be the wrong move. You'll get to the end of your day and look at the accumulation of things you have done and wish you'd stayed in bed. Some days it will be the right move. You'll have a smile on your face and a skip in your step and life will look rosy. But on a lot of days we decide not to decide and just let life have our move. There is no such thing as a 'pass turn' in the game of life. Each day is going to happen whether you want it to or not, and if you don't take your move when it is your turn then someone or something else will take it for you.

Don't decide not to play. The end of the game is very dismal for those who decide to sit it out. And now we come to a very serious issue, and one that will cause many of you to hesitate before proceeding—your education.

Gaining Knowledge

* * * * * * * * * * * * *

THERE COMES A TIME IN a mother's life when she gets to wrap up her first child in a school uniform or at least some form of smart school clothes, give them a packed lunch, bundle them into the car or bus or just walk with them, and take them to school or pre-school or whatever it is called in your part of the world. She makes sure they are settled, says goodbye, maybe with a wistful tear, especially on the first day, and a new phase of their lives has begun.

Now flip that over to the child, who, on this Journey, is you and me. It's fun at first—maybe, or maybe not. There are nice teachers and nice fellow pupils, but there are also scary things out there. But even if conditions are totally rosy, sooner or later, you come face to face with the fact that you are in this strange new place to gain knowledge. It comes as a rude shock to some that it actually matters that 3 comes immediately after 2 and that it makes a difference which way round you draw the letter 'e'.

It starts slowly and subtly at first, but just like the famous 'frog in the pot', the heat is gradually turned up until before long you have been introduced to the delights of 'homework', 'essays' and 'tests'. Some of you just ate this part of your life for breakfast. Some of you found it to be a form of torture dressed up in the guise of civilisation. Whether you endured it or enjoyed it, we all had some form of education.

Your Journey of gaining knowledge began much earlier than this. As I've already pointed out, you used your taste buds to start learning from a very early age. This new phase, however, is both structured and somewhat enforced. Taste buds are still involved, of course. School lunches are hardly a culinary delight, and you learn that food can be quite boring when you have the same thing every day. But by now, the other four senses are heavily involved, especially hearing.

Then there is another 'sense' that gets pressure put on it for the first time and that is thinking. Remember the first time the teacher asked you a question that you didn't know the answer to because you were daydreaming instead of listening? All of a sudden your brain went into panic mode and either a stupid answer, or just plain 'I don't know', pops out and as everyone laughs at you, the desire for the earth to open up and swallow you enters your experience! Some of you even took the decision, consciously or unconsciously, at that point, to become the class clown as a survival mechanism.

The process of schooling or education is a rather strange one. For some, the ritual of spoon feeding them with facts and principles that they must learn by rote is exactly what the doctor ordered. Traditional education, however, tends not to handle the fact the people have vastly different learning styles and vastly different motivators. I knew someone whose husband had been labelled 'dumb' at school and dropped out as soon as he could. However he was an avid reader of car magazines and could quote endless facts and vital statistics about cars, on demand. He was not 'dumb', he was just not motivated to learn in the traditional way, or to study numbers and kings and places and chemicals. He liked cars.

It is an oft repeated fact that great and successful men, such as Henry Ford, frequently had virtually no schooling. Ford was not an ignorant man, and he was only uneducated in the sense that his formal schooling was minimal. But many wrote him off as being uneducated despite his great success. Albert Einstein was unquestionably a genius, and yet he had a rocky relationship with traditional education. He completed his schooling via quite a circuitous route. This should encourage you if you have had your own schooling interrupted by circumstances or poor choices.

So what is the big deal about going to school anyway?

My eldest son had a struggle with maths—he wanted to know how to multiply when he was just four. My wife, who was full time mother at that stage, decided that he really needed to go to school and pushed to get him an early intake at a school that didn't take early intakes! This was fine for a while until it became apparent that, while he was academically achieving, he was suffering socially because of the age difference, however small it was. On one occasion when changing cities, states and school systems, we held him back a year in a way that was pretty transparent to him, and I think it was a wise choice.

The point that this brings up about school is that it is not just an academic activity. It is also a social activity. We gain different kinds of friends and different kinds of enemies at school. We learn to relate to different adults and to relate to adults in a different way. We get buttons pushed that we didn't even know we had! You can probably remember your first school fight, whether you were the cause or the victim, and maybe your first walk to the principal's office. I certainly remember mine.

Anyone who has had, as I did, first hand experience with a school bully, will appreciate the early understanding that not everyone on the world is going to be nice to you. For some, the trauma of that bullying experience influences a lot of what goes on in later life. We'll come to more of that in a minute, but suffice it to say that our interaction with bullies deeply impacts our view of what it takes to survive life. Sometimes we fear that we won't.

On the positive side, school instils in us a sense of society that will help us to relate to the 'real' world. In school there are authorities, challenges, opportunities to both succeed and fail, relationships, rewards, punishments, goals; just about everything that we will face in life we run up against in those first few critical years. We may not enjoy the process in every respect but it is certainly valuable. Whatever knowledge we gain is, to some degree, incidental. It is the experience we gain that really matters.

Because of school, our Journey through life begins to take two roughly parallel courses—our life at school and our life at home. This is a pattern that will continue through the rest of our lives for many of us. As we step off the end of our education into some form of employment we maintain this dual mode of living. As a result, we actually develop a kind of schizophrenia in that we develop a school personality and a school identity that is different from our home personality and identity.

For some people the two can be worlds apart. A person who is quite bold at home can end up being shy and retiring at school. Sometimes the model citizen at home can be quite the tearaway at school. This world of education enables and sometimes even encourages us to do something that we may not have thought to do before—and that is to wear a mask. We develop a persona that is not our natural persona and appear to people the way we want to appear.

Masks are a very interesting part of life. We put them on for a variety of reasons. We use them to gain the attention of people whom we want to impress. Many a boy or girl gets to see who the opposite sex wants them to see for the purposes of dating. If the masks are never penetrated, there can be severe trouble later on in the relationship. We also use them to hide behind when we want to prevent people from seeing who we really are. Sometimes we use them to hide even from ourselves. From there, they can develop into something quite tragic—walls.

Masks are for hiding or disguising. Walls are for defence. When we put up a wall, it means we are no longer engaging with life from a point of view of trying to achieve or relate or survive. As soon as we put up a wall, we are at war. What is on the other side of that wall is the enemy. Not everyone who engages with life as a combatant puts up walls. But everyone who puts up a wall accepts defeat from the outset. Walls are the beginning of long term failure. Bullying, as mentioned before, can do a lot of damage in this process. Bullies can encourage us to put up larger, more secure walls to make sure we don't get hurt, but then hurt comes in so many different forms and the subtler forms of hurt can make even more formidable walls.

The biggest things that hold us back in life are the walls we put up. Walls keep out people who can help us along life's Journey as well as keeping out the 'bad' people. Even when we manage to find a relationship after putting up a wall, we usually don't get the full benefit of the relationship and we rob the other person. Then we start to accumulate emotional baggage. The great thing about walls is that they can be torn down. Baggage can be left behind. It's never easy, but it is worth it.

The Journey through school, high school, college, university and whatever other educational avenues we take can be a long one. During that time we develop walls, masks and all kinds of other baggage that we take along with us. Many of us develop most of our biggest traumas in school. Yet despite all of this, the majority of us come out of the educational process as better people. Either despite or because of our education we emerge from the process ready for life in some sense of being ready.

For some of us we develop lifelong friendships, find heroes in some of our teachers, meet our future spouses, find careers, decide on life goals and develop our dreams. The process of gaining knowledge yields us enduring rewards. You probably forgot most of what you learned in school, but you probably have never forgotten some of the people who have influenced you along the way. The memory of those people and sometimes relationships with those people can carry you through your darkest days.

Probably the most important thing you learn or perhaps fail to learn during your process of becoming educated, however, is how to acquire knowledge. People like Henry Ford who had little formal schooling learned how to acquire knowledge. They learned to surround themselves with people who could give them knowledge or how to use reference material or, in this day and age, how to surf the web! It doesn't really matter what you don't know as long as you know how to find out. Then the only thing that stands in your way is laziness.

Gaining knowledge is, in itself, a Journey, and the biggest mistake anyone can make is to stop that process when school stops. Anyone who has gone on to any form of higher education realises that as the process goes on, you are spoon fed less and less until by the time you get to do a PhD, you have to do all the work yourself. When we stop learning we start to die, usually accompanied with copious amounts of TV. When we keep learning, we keep moving forward and that process never has to stop.

Don't ever despise your school days. Whether you loved them or hated them, those days are an important part of who you are. You will never change what has happened, but as you look at what you experienced, how you reacted to those things, how you changed and what masks and walls you used to cope, you can better understand the way you react now and why you interact with life and the people you meet in the way that you do. Try not to think of any of it as good or bad. Just accept that it was what it was and that now you have the opportunity to do what your education prepared you for—learn.

Take all of your educational experience and learn from it. Make the most of the process you went through, whether you dropped out of High School or completed a PhD, and realise that, whatever else it did, it prepared you for life. Sure you may not have finished that preparation, but there are people in the world who would desperately like even as much as you did, yet have no access to it. Your education did all that it could do for you and without it, you would not be where you are. The people you have met, the fun you have had, the principles you hold to, mostly stem from your school days.

Now we come to a part of our Journey that perhaps we'd like to forget. That's the part where things didn't quite go to plan.

Traps and Pitfalls

※ ※ ※ ※ ※ ※ ※ ※ ※ ※ ※ ※ ※

THINGS HAPPEN. GOOD THINGS AND bad things. They started when Mum gave us sweets. They started when we were very young when we tripped and hurt ourselves. Sometimes however, a truly bad thing happens, that threatens to end our world. Sometimes we call these tragedies. The loss of a loved one. Destruction of our home in a fire or natural disaster. Sometimes they are just devastating life incidents like being made redundant from our job with no hope of a new one.

Sometimes life is just hard. That statement is very relative. In the comfortable western world, it can mean having to buy beans for dinner instead of steak. In many parts of the world it can mean the half bowl of rice that you had for breakfast having to last for two days instead of one. Or much worse. I recently reflected that while we in the UK were lamenting over two women who had been killed by a taxi driver, in the Ivory Coast, Libya and Syria, bodies were being piled up in the streets because of civil war. Whatever 'life is hard' means for you, it is still true.

A former Australian Prime Minister by the name of Malcolm Fraser was asked by a woman who had many difficulties in life, what his government would do for her. He famously remarked "Life wasn't meant to be easy." He was referring to a quote by George Bernard Shaw, *"Life wasn't meant to be easy, my child, but take courage: it can be delightful!"* I don't know if he intended to quote the whole thing, but he never got the chance. He became a laughing stock ever after. I'm not sure that if he had gotten the whole thing out that it would have made a difference.

Like so many people, because of her difficult circumstances, this woman wanted answers, wanted someone to blame, wanted somehow to make sense of what she had been through. She maybe even wanted lies to make her feel better. She did not want to be told the plain simple truth that is sometimes expressed in the vernacular as "Life sucks." I don't believe that is the whole story, but on one level it is true. This world is a messed up place that sometimes gives you lemons and salt just to rub in your wounds. And being told to make lemonade somehow just doesn't seem to comfort you!

Unless you have only been around for a very short time, you probably know what I am talking about. I lost my younger brother to a brain aneurism when he was just a young father. I didn't get to say anything to him. He was just gone. Also I have been made redundant from my job twice and spent long intervals unemployed. Having said both of these, many of you will be able to recount much worse things! Terminal illnesses, loss of multiple loved ones, major loss of property, income, respectability and so on.

So all of that has happened and maybe worse, but what about you? What happened to your Journey after the tragedy or disaster? I always remember the story of a student pilot who was in a single-engine, two-seater light plane, with his instructor beside him. Suddenly, the engine cut out and the student, in a panic, turned to the instructor and said "What are we going to do? What are we going to do?" The instructor calmly replied, "We're going to land." And they did. Whatever the final outcome, gravity was going to have its way and they had an appointment with the ground. Some people use the phrase "This too will pass," and whatever you are feeling when disaster strikes, it is mostly true.

Whatever happens to you, life has just made its move, and in the rules of the game, that means it's your turn. How are you going to react? What are you going to do? There are many choices, and we have seen a lot of people make so many of them that we hardly need to do research to find out what they are. On one extreme, there is suicide and some take that course all too readily. At the other there is the sponge, who takes it all in and bottles it all up for later. In between there is a range of options both positive and negative, although far too few people take positive options.

I have already mentioned a passage in the Bible that most people are familiar with, even those who have never darkened the door of a church. The 23rd Psalm contains this verse:—

Yea, though I walk through the valley of the shadow of death, I will fear no evil: for thou art with me; thy rod and thy staff they comfort me. (Verse 4, King James Version)

Notice two words in there that make all the difference: 'walk through'. The valley of the shadow of death is familiar to many of us, but it is not a place for camping in. Unfortunately the camping grounds there are well populated with the tents of those who decided that they belong there, or deserve to be there, or would just rather be there than move on.

There are many reasons why you might want to camp in the valley of the shadow of death. For some who are suffering grief, they do not wish to dishonour the memory of a loved one, so they put their lives on hold for fear of losing the last link to a lost love or a fond partnership. Others find the misery and suffering in some strange way familiar and easier to handle than taking on the responsibility of getting on with life. Whatever the reason, their Journey has come to an end, at least in that area. I sincerely hope that yours has not!

This brings us to one of the most commonly used excuses for simply camping around a negative life experience—blaming God. It's surprising how many people who claim not to believe in God will actually blame Him for what they've been through. It's not rational, but very little around grief and negative experience is ever rational. It all comes of the desire to have someone to blame, someone to pin it on so it all somehow makes sense. If we can blame God or the government or UFOs, then it makes it all so much easier to take.

I want to suggest to you, however, that the real problem is not with whatever has made the bad thing happen, or with the bad thing itself. It all revolves around how we react to it. It is very easy to illustrate the point by imagining a room full of people of diverse ages and backgrounds and musical tastes. I walk into the room with an MP3 player and hit the play button. The first track I play is a heavy metal track. Now have a look at the people in the room. Some are smiling. Some are moving to the music (probably not gentle swaying!). Some are covering their ears.

Now I play the second track. This one is "Ave Maria". Notice how the expressions change! The ones who were smiling are now rolling their eyes. The ones who were moving are getting ready to move out of the room. And the ones who had their ears covered are listening to this one. Some are even streaming tears down their faces.

Notice that in each case, everybody heard the same music. Why didn't they all react the same way? Because they are all different you say, but why are they different? Everyone in the room had the choice to react to the music any way they wanted to. I like neither of those genres, but if I let myself, I can understand and appreciate both, without enjoying them. It's a choice I make. Musical taste is a result of a series of choices in listening that have led you to a current 'conclusion' about what you like and what you don't care for.

The same is true of any life experience. Helen Keller is not the only person to have been deaf, dumb and blind, so why did she react the way she did to that terrifying life experience, and others just suffer with it? I don't blame anyone for suffering—but Helen's life response was just that—a response, and anyone can respond. Was Douglas Bader made of sterner stuff than others who lost their legs in wartime such that he not only walked again, but flew? Or was it just that he made a different choice than the other amputees made?

If you don't know Helen Keller or Douglas Bader then I am probably just betraying my age, in which case I have one word to say to you: Google! Substitute any names you like in there, the effect is the same. I won't pretend that any such choice is easy. It takes a lot of guts to stare at the ruins of your life's work, having lost all you have known and everyone you loved, and deciding to carry on anyway. If you've been there and haven't made that choice I don't blame you one bit. But you are missing out on life.

Before moving on I want to address a subject that I have already touched on and that is the role of God in all of this. As I've already said, God often cops the blame for anything bad that happens, even if He doesn't exist! However He also gets accused of not existing on the basis that the disaster has happened!

"If there is a God of Love, why do the innocent suffer?"

If there is no God of Love, what makes them innocent and who cares if they suffer?

I don't know where I first heard this, but it is very profound. God's non-existence does not explain the suffering of the innocent any more than His existence, along with the suffering, proves that He caused it. I don't want to get into a complete argument about the existence of God here but just suppose for a minute that God didn't exist. Does that help you to get over the tragedy any more than believing that He exists and that He may be at fault? Long before you get around to considering God's role in what has happened to you, take a look at the choices you have made that led you there.

"Well, I didn't choose for my mother to die!!"

Neither did I choose for my brother to die, but I did choose not to call him a few days before his untimely death. I had the thought, "Call Paul, you haven't talked to him for a while," and I didn't. So now I have a choice. Do I blame God for taking my brother? No, I chose to beat myself up because I didn't call. Then I was faced with other choices. How long was I going to beat myself up? Was I going to let the lesson I learned there affect my behaviour? Was I going to 'seize the day' and live my life differently?

So far I have only talked about things that have happened to you. What about ways that you have gone astray directly because of your choices? Examples that come to mind are, getting involved in gambling to excess, drinking to excess, having an affair, stealing, physical violence, even murder! Some of these things may get padded around with excuses. Your husband didn't give you any attention so you had an affair with a friend who gave you inappropriate attention. Your parents always criticised you so you rebelled and took up a life of crime. It was still your choice.

The issue with these pitfalls is that they tend to ensnare you for a long period of time. Once you have made a choice of this nature it becomes so much easier to continue to make negative choices and spiral down further into the mire. It's like an ex-smoker who has one cigarette in a moment of weakness. Since she's smoked one, she may as well finish the pack! At the end of the pack it is so easy to justify buying another. Once a person has stolen, it becomes so much easier to steal again. The first illicit liaison with a member of the opposite sex removes 99% of the inhibition of doing it again.

The great thing about getting to the point where you accept that it is now your move and it is up to you if things are going to change, is that you are once more in the driver's seat. You are no longer allowing life to take you where it wants you to go. You may not be absolutely certain of where your Journey is going to turn to next, but you've pulled up stakes, packed up your tent and decided to move again. The valley of the shadow of death is no longer your home.

If grief has been your jailer, you now have the choice to live your life for the living instead of for the dead. While you have been stuck, people have been suffering for the lack of your input into their lives. It may be children who have been longing to see you smile again. It may be a husband who wants your affection instead of watching you pining for a lost child that you can never bring back. I am not suggesting for one instant that you should forget about the loved one you have lost. You should honour their memory by getting on with your life—if they truly loved you, they would be very sad to see you putting your life on hold because of them.

If on the other hand, a bad life choice has held you back, such as drug abuse, your choice to get treatment, support and a new start in life is the only way to reverse that bad choice. It may be a thousand miles to get back to where you were. Maybe you don't even need to get back there. Depending on how bad things have been for you, you probably have a pretty clean slate to work with. It's not an easy road ahead, but you have a lot to offer, and the world has been waiting for you to get back in the stream of life.

I could go through countless possibilities but by now, hopefully, you get the picture. So now, as we resume our Journey, we will go into an area that affects all of us but so many of us neglect for most of our lives—our spiritual Journey.

Changing Destinations

* * * * * * * * * * * * *

ILIKE TRAINS. I ALSO LIKE train stations. European train stations, particularly Italian ones, fascinate me because you get to see whole rows of trains all ready to go somewhere. Who knows where the people that pile onto them are headed? I once made a train Journey that involved three changes of trains. I started at 2AM at a station that was locked and the doors were unlocked by the security guard to let me board. My first change was at 3AM where I had to wait on a deserted platform again inside a locked station, for an hour and a half with only a sleeping drunk to accompany me!

The point of the story is that at each station I made a change of train because I wanted to change directions. The destination of the first train was London. My ultimate destination was Newhaven so I could catch a ferry to Dieppe in France. If I had stayed on the first train, I would have ended up in London, and missed my ferry. There's nothing wrong with a visit to London, but I would have missed joining up with my team in Dieppe!

Sometimes, however, the change of destinations is necessary to avoid a situation that is truly not where you want to go. Suppose I am on a train that is heading into a war zone, or a hurricane or a forest fire? I would definitely want to get off that train and change destinations. There are a lot of better alternatives than one of those! Probably not too many of us have been on a train in that sort of circumstance, but I am sure you have read the stories or seen the movies.

So far all I have talked about has been The Journey. I have not mentioned destinations, but there is no Journey without one. You can go for a stroll in the park and end up where you started, but the Journey that we are on has a definite end point. Many people would rather avoid this subject, but there is a destination in this life, and whatever direction you are travelling, it does have an end point.

Sometimes we make major changes of direction such as selecting a new career, getting married, getting divorced, changing countries, having children, either naturally or by other means such as adoption. Some of these can happen as a result of a crisis such as has been mentioned in the previous chapter. The change of direction that I am particularly interested in here though is of a different nature.

Ponce de León famously discovered Florida while searching for the Fountain of Youth. Whether this is truth or legend, it still illustrates an important principle. The idea that somehow we can cheat aging and thereby cheat death has fascinated many people down through the ages. Fascinating it may have been, but successful it was not! The real reason for this obsession is to avoid having to deal with the reality that we will arrive one day at our destination.

So let's look at some destinations:—

For many, at the end of this life there is nothing. You simply breathe your last, close your eyes, and then there is nothing. Kind of like an eternal dreamless sleep. That's not much of a destination in my thinking, but it does give you an incentive to hang onto life for all it's worth and live it hard and fast! After all, if this life is all there is, then there's no point wasting it! Not that it has that general effect. Instead it just means that there is just no hope at the end of a meaningless life. It takes more than a vague resignation to eternal nothingness to motivate people to live life differently.

Then there's the rather odd idea of getting your body frozen when you die in the hope that someone in the future will find a way to cure whatever you died of and bring you back to life. This is just another variant on Ponce de León's search for eternal youth. This is all about avoiding the issue of a destination at all. If we can somehow keep the Journey going on forever we don't even have to think about a destination. No matter how desperate and last ditch this idea is, it at least creates the illusion of taking the sting out of death.

Another idea that some subscribe to is that we get to the end our lives and we become freed from our body, able to wander the universe at will, no longer shackled by physical limitations. This is especially attractive if we have been afflicted by some severely constricting ailment such as paraplegia or other form or paralysis. I toyed with this idea for a long time, but had no real basis for believing it, it was just a fanciful notion for me.

Reincarnation is a perennial favourite, although more often referred to in jest in the Western world than believed in reality. Whether you believe you will come back as another human, or that you have to go through being higher or lower animals, this is more a deferral of destination than a complete avoidance. Usually the ultimate end of reincarnation is some kind of nirvana or place of eternal peace but the Journey goes on through different bodies until you get to that place.

Now I'm going to cover the two traditional alternatives: Heaven and hell. And I do believe in both of these, just so there's no ambiguity regarding my position. I would warn you to look away now if you don't want to be offended, but I rather hope that you will decide to carry on and share this part of the Journey with me. I am not apologising for my beliefs, but I will offer you the choice.

The thing about Heaven and hell is that there is something of the 'carrot and stick' mentality about it. "If you're good, you'll go to Heaven; if you're bad you'll go to hell." There are two unhelpful pictures that I want to deal with before I go any further.

Firstly there is the picture of Heaven with everyone sitting around on clouds playing harps and nothing else to do. It is a place of indolence and not much better than the idea of just going to sleep. No-one really wants to go to a place like that. You can only think of it as a boring place if that's your picture. My picture of Heaven is not so filled with detail, as much as it is with delight. My view of Heaven is a place that is so amazingly wonderful that it is not possible to be unhappy. Every moment is a delight. Boredom is unthinkable.

Secondly there is the picture of hell that is accompanied with the comment, "Oh, I may as well go to hell when I die because all my mates will be there and we can have a good time together." This is the view that hell isn't really all that bad a place, it's just a bit warm. My view of hell is a place that is so unthinkably terrifying that every moment is an eternity of torment. It is a place to be avoided at all costs. It is, in fact, a very bad place.

Given those choices it's no surprise that many of us make our Journey under either a fear of hell, a hope of Heaven or a mixture of both. Many people also have a vague general hope that they'll end up in Heaven one day as long as they've been good—or at least not too bad. That's a bit like getting on any old train and sort of hoping that you end up in London, as long as you've paid the fare, or at least most of it! You'd never dream of taking a physical Journey like that so why would you think of doing your spiritual Journey in that way?

To my way of thinking you need to make a decision from an early stage what sort of destination you want to aim for, and make the Journey accordingly. With my hypothetical Journey to London it makes a big difference what train I get on in the first place. If I get on a train that will take me to Manchester, there's not much hope of somehow miraculously ending up in London. But even if I get on a train that is heading towards London, if I don't take notice of the train change announcements, I could still end up somewhere else.

That is why I called this chapter "Changing Destinations". This is about listening for the train change announcements in life that will allow us to get on the right train to get to our London. This may come in the form of a street preacher, or a friend who has found a strange peace, or a pamphlet that mysteriously finds its way into our hands. Because I would like to put it to you that, since our grandcestors were kicked out of that Garden so many centuries ago, we have been headed in the wrong direction.

I would like to suggest that the traditional picture of a God 'sending' people to hell is all wrong. He is not sending, we are going. He is rescuing. I won't try to justify that statement; it is a conclusion I have come to after years of study and experience. However it puts a very different perspective on life. If you were trapped in a burning building, and someone came along and told you the safe way to an exit, you would be very wise to change directions, especially if you were heading the opposite way. If we were to view Heaven as the safe way out and hell as the heart of the fire in the burning building, then it makes our view of spiritual destinations very different.

There is always someone who will try to make Heaven and hell just metaphors for being at peace and being in turmoil, and if that's working for you, I won't argue, but from my perspective, this idea of a rescue from a bad situation that wasn't even meant for us, makes so much more sense. The idea of a God who is capriciously punishing some and blessing others doesn't add up. Why bother with all that when He could have just wiped out Adam and Eve when they ate the fruit? It's just an excuse to blame God for things that are more likely just to be the result of choices we have made.

However, I would like to put to you another possibility in the midst of all this talk about destinations. Everything I have said so far is about destinations as places. Heaven, hell, nirvana, London, Manchester. Sometimes we go to a city like London because we want to see the sights, but sometimes, we go there for a very different reason. I have been to Manchester several times for a visit to one of my daughters. Why Manchester?

Because that's where she lives! If she'd lived in Glasgow, that's where I would have gone.

What if our destination is not a place at all, but rather a Person? What if all along, it has never been about 'where' we are going, but rather about Who we are going to see? That's why we are once more going to go Under a Tree.

Under a Tree (again)

❋ ❋ ❋ ❋ ❋ ❋ ❋ ❋ ❋ ❋ ❋ ❋ ❋

I BEGAN THIS BOOK WITH A story about a Garden and a Tree. That, I contended, is where our Journey began. We were driven from that Garden, and that Tree, and now we are going to visit a very different Garden and a very different Tree. If you don't identify with this part of my Journey, that's fine, but please keep coming with me and see what I have to show you. I hope that you will identify when we are done with this chapter.

In the first chapter I introduced you to the start of all of our Journeys, when our ancestors, Adam and Eve were expelled from the Garden that we all, in a sense, are striving to return to. However there was another Garden that another Adam visited and we will now visit it with Him. This Garden is dark, it is on a rather barren hillside, but it is full of olive trees, and it has a name—Gethsemane. In this Garden as we stand, a bit unsure of what we are seeing, a Man enters with a somewhat ragtag band of eleven followers and engages in conversation with them.

After His words, he takes three of the men and withdraws deeper into the Garden, leaving the other eight behind. We follow cautiously, hardly daring to breathe, lest we disturb what is happening. After a while He turns and addresses the three, and they settle down on the ground as He moves a short distance away. What happens next looks like the Man is engaged in earnest prayer. On two occasions He returns to the three. The first time, seeing them asleep, He arouses them, and speaks in a stern voice. The second time, after another period of prayer, He returns to them and speaks again, but not enough to arouse them this time—He just lets them sleep.

Finally, He arises, looking exhausted from His supplications, and we see on His face dark markings, as if some sort of staining liquid has run down from His forehead. He addresses the three sharply again, arouses them one more time, and they make to leave. By this time you have noticed the flickering lights of a few naked-flame torches coming up the hill, being borne by an unseen group of people.

As the Man and the three move to rejoin the other eight, the flame bearing group comes into view. You can now see them to be a squad of soldiers, led by a man dressed much like one of the Man's followers. The group arrives at the meeting of the Man and His followers. The plainly dressed man who is leading the soldiers approaches the Man and kisses Him on the cheek in the manner of the greetings of many cultures.

What follows is confusing. At one stage the soldiers all fall down, but the Man does not flee. A sword is drawn and a man is struck, but somehow the situation seems to remain in the Man's control. However the end of it all is that the Man is led, bound by the soldiers, and taken back down the hill and into the city on the hill facing this one. Most of the followers disperse for fear that they too will be taken into custody, having been completely unnerved by the whole incident. However a couple of them follow at a safe distance.

The events of this night are well documented, but that incident in the Garden had as profound an impact on our destinies as the other event in the first Garden so may centuries before. In that time in the Garden, this Man committed Himself to God's Will in earnest prayer and the battle for your soul entered its final phase. Because in that commitment, the Man, known by so many as Jesus the Christ, committed Himself to paying the price for our freedom.

As well as a Garden, I promised you a Tree. We will get there, but the significance of Jesus' simple words at that encounter with God, "Not My will but Yours be done," meant that the end of our banishment from God's presence was about to be accomplished. People tend to gloss over this part of the story of our Journey as being less important than what was to follow. But the dark stain that was on His forehead that night was blood and it is with His Blood that He paid the price for our ancestor Adam's rebellion.

This is not a theological treatise, so I will not attempt to explain why all of this was necessary. This is a Journey, and I wanted you to see this Man, whom we will see again shortly, decide that, in His Journey, you were worth the price that He had to pay, if that is what God required. Had He not made that choice, we would not be making this Journey. A very different course of history would have ensued but there is no point speculating on what it would have been.

The next day, we again see this Man, Jesus, making a Journey that no man should have to take, but we will take it with Him, because we have an appointment with Him at the end of it. Now He is not just stained on His forehead. His entire body is bloodied and beaten. To look at Him you would be forgiven for wondering why He has not already died from loss of blood. He is carrying a heavy wooden beam, and He is so weak that someone is selected from the watching crowd and compelled by the attending soldiers to carry the timber for Him.

The Journey is long, slow and agonising. Will He make it? Yes, He will because He already decided in the Garden that He would make it. That is now the only reason He is still alive, because He has an appointment with you and I on the top of a hill. He ascends that hill slowly as it leers at Him with its skull-like appearance, and He is thrust down roughly onto a cross-shaped structure completed by the beam He was carrying and now brought by an apparently innocent bystander.

After being nailed onto the wood through His hands and feet, the whole structure is roughly hauled into an upright position and dropped into a hole, as His body cries out in agony with every cruel movement. Finally, He is there, looking down on you as you stand at the foot of a crude wooden cross with Him nailed to it, a cruel parody of a Tree, but a Tree nonetheless. This is the Tree I promised you. You may be forgiven for thinking that it has nothing to do with the other Tree, but it has everything to do with it.

At each side of this cross you see another cross, each holding another man, two criminals crucified alongside this Man, Jesus, whom we have been following. At the first Tree a choice was made that started your Journey outside the Garden. Now, another choice is going to be made that could change your Journey forever. At first, these two criminals are hurling abuse at Jesus. "If you are who you say you are, take us down from these crosses!" But as the day progresses, the attitude of one changes.

As the pain-driven tirade of abuse comes from one man, the other begins to realise that the Man in the middle is no ordinary man. "We are here because of our crimes. We deserve this punishment. But this Man has done no wrong." He recognises something that many in His day did not perceive: He had lived His life perfectly without the sin and failure that characterises all of our lives.

He then turns to Jesus and says something that changes his seemingly hopeless future. "Lord, remember me when You are come into Your Kingdom." And Jesus receives him. The choice is the same choice. Do we stretch forth our hands for the forbidden Tree or for the Tree of life? This criminal made a choice that took him home. The other made a choice that many continue to make—railing at God and His Son, instead of asking for His help.

We hear it all the time—"Why do You let the innocent suffer?", "Why did You take my child?", "Why do You send earthquakes, floods, famines?", "Why, why, why?" We are too busy appealing to Him to take us off our own cross, when all He wants us to do is to ask Him to receive us. As long as we insist on being 'right' and demanding answers from He who owes us no answers, we will continue to suffer. Once we surrender to His mercy, our suffering ends.

I have, of course, brought you to this place because I want you to make that choice. If you already have, then I am happy for you. You can continue on this Journey with me, confident in the knowledge that one day, we will be with Him. If you have not, then I encourage you, even urge you, not just to dismiss this as the wild ravings of a religious lunatic. If you doubt that this Man has the power to receive you, then take the time to get to know Him. Read His book. Meet more of His people.

However if you believe what I have told you, and understand that this Jesus is the One Who is showing us the way out of the burning building into safety, then turn to Him now and say, as the criminal did, "Lord, remember me when You are come into Your Kingdom." In other words, "Lord, receive me into Your Kingdom."

As you walk down from the hill, leaving Jesus to breathe His last, the events of the day seem like a defeat, despite the promise of Paradise, but in three days, He will come out of His own grave to prove that death has no more power over Him, nor over anyone who is in His Kingdom. Your destination has changed, and so has your life.

There is a saying that goes "I used to chop wood and carry water. Then I received enlightenment. Now I chop wood and carry water." This decision is much like that. You will go back to the same life you had before, the same family, live in the same house, but now, the destination of your Journey has changed. Now you are going Home, not to the original Garden, but to a new Garden and a new Tree, the Tree of life.

As we resume our Journey, however, sometimes we start to wander a bit.

Wandering Around

※ ※ ※ ※ ※ ※ ※ ※ ※ ※ ※ ※ ※

A FEW THOUSAND YEARS AGO, A million or more people left Egypt in a hurry, led by a man named Moses. There was a heart stopping moment when Pharaoh nearly killed them all, but a walk through a valley of water in the Red Sea put paid to Pharaoh's intentions and they were home free—in a desert! There was now just a short Journey—a matter of weeks—from there to their ultimate goal—the land of Canaan. That Journey took them forty years.

The reason that I introduce this story into the discussion of our Journey, is that the story of the exodus from Egypt is, as well as being a 100% true literal story, a parable of our own escape from eternal death into eternal Life. Even as we have made the choice at the foot of the Tree in the last Chapter to pursue His offer of freedom, so the Children of Israel took up God's offer by joining in the Passover. Within a very short time, they were once again in trouble.

The incident that caused the biggest trouble was what happened when they actually reached their goal. They sent spies into Canaan to check out the new premises. The report was that the lodgings were great, but the current tenants were too much for them. They said 'we are as grasshoppers in their eyes and in our own eyes'. They judged themselves to be too small to take hold of what God was giving them and so God said, 'OK, you can just stay here in this wilderness until the next generation grows up to inherit it—if you are too small, your kids will be big enough'.

I am paraphrasing of course, but you get the general idea. In modern terms, they got to the brink of achieving their goal, and they sabotaged it. Then they were condemned to wander around for 40 years. They were still on their Journey, but now they were in a holding pattern and were not moving forwards or backwards. They were literally waiting to die, there was nothing else for them to do. The kids who were going to grow up to inherit Canaan were also waiting for their parents to die. And by this time, their grandkids were starting to be born so three generations of Israelites were tied up because the first generation missed it.

Life consists of a series of opportunities. These are as simple as the opportunity to get up at 6 AM and pray or meditate instead of getting up at 7AM and just having a shower before leaving for work. Sometimes they are much greater opportunities like the opportunity to step into a place where we can make a real difference in the world we live in. We have a habit of missing opportunities, caused as much by our blindness to them as our unwillingness to acknowledge them.

When we miss a small opportunity, we usually get the opportunity to do it over and over again. The big opportunities tend to come along a lot less frequently, so we wander. People who miss the opportunity to gain the education that will enable them to do what they really want to do, wander by either drifting from job to job, or getting stuck with a job that they hate. Or even worse, they become homeless vagabonds, drifting from place to place.

The thing about literal homeless people, is that we look down our noses at them, with the 'holier than thou' mindset that just says 'get a job, you loser!', all the while failing to see that we are often just as homeless as they are. Oh, sure, we have a house and a wife or husband and kids and a job but we are still wandering. The Journey has become, for us, just a grind. It is a survival mission in which the aim of each day is just to get to the end of it and sleep, hoping beyond hope that somehow the next day is going to be better.

I am probably sounding depressing. If I go on like this I might even depress myself. But the truth is, we've probably all been there. We Journey whether we like it or not. The Israelites did not simply camp at the border of Canaan when they missed their calling, they wandered in the desert. Life in some form or another carried on for them. They were still on a Journey. They still had an appointment with the Promised Land. The time of the appointment had been shifted—by forty years.

Thankfully, we are seldom put in the place of being forced to wander for four decades. When we miss it, there is usually another place at which we can resume the Journey at a point that allows us to move forward instead of just wandering. However there are quite a few of us who can count the times we have spent wandering in decades. Take the time to look at your own wanderings. Can you identify the point at which you missed the 'drop-off' point, so to speak, and ended up in a rut? There are usually regrets associated with such a point, and I want to talk more about regrets in the next chapter, but their presence is a good indicator of where the path took a less than helpful turn on your Journey.

Let's take a look at some examples. A young woman wants a career as a journalist. She does the study, and while at University, she falls head over heels in love with someone. They get married, have children, and she puts her career on hold. It happens very often. By the time the children go to school, she thinks of maybe restarting her career, but of course part time working options in some careers are a pipe dream. So, she settles for motherhood. Motherhood is an excellent career choice, but it isn't what she wanted. She wanders.

A man starts his own business and, as so many businesses do, it starts well but then things go wrong. His business folds and so he decides to get employment so that he can clear his debts and get enough capital to start over. Only he never seems to get enough capital and never gets around to starting over. So, he settles for the daily grind of a job he hates and figures that is just his lot in life. If he had been meant for business he would have made it the first time, so he gives in to 'fate'. He wanders.

None of this is about being right or wrong. It's not wrong to be a full time mum or an employee or any other of a thousand things that you might have found yourself doing. It's just a crying shame if that's not what you wanted to do. The Journey is about direction, and it's great to take a detour every now and again to see something you've never seen, but if the Journey doesn't have a destination then it's just a ramble.

There is, however, an interesting twist to this. We are multi-faceted beings. We can have a direction totally sorted in one area of our lives and yet be completely directionless in another. Take the man who has his business sorted and is making a million a year, but his family life is in tatters or he has no relationship while deep down he longs for one. Or the woman who has a great career, great home, well behaved kids and loving husband but is on the brink of a nervous breakdown trying to juggle everything to keep it all that way.

We have many lives that we engage with on our Journey. We have a purely physical life that involves our health, our fitness, our physical appearance and our five senses. Then we have our mental life or our thought life. There is our spiritual life, our relationship with God. There is also our financial life and our social life. All of these areas require a direction, for the whole person to be on the Journey in some kind of harmony.

By this time you might be thinking, "Aaagh! How can I think of so many things at once?" The great thing is, you don't have to! Even as you have been reading this, unless you have a really good balance of those five areas, you've probably become conscious of one main area where you have been wandering for a while. If your relationships are great but your fitness bothers you, then just keep doing what you are doing with your social life and focus on the physical aspects of your life.

The other side to this is that I am not talking about fixing everything. I am just talking about direction. Without direction we are wandering. With direction we are on our Journey. You might feel that you are a thousand miles from the fitness level that you desire, but a Journey of a thousand miles begins with a single step. As soon as you decide, and I mean really decide, that you want to improve your fitness level, then you have direction and how you get there is largely immaterial.

It is possible to have direction, but for that direction to be the wrong way. I'm not talking about someone who is careless about their relationships or their finances or their health. I am talking about someone who has become bent on self destruction. Someone who is wilfully drinking themselves into an early grave, or gambling themselves into poverty. At its extreme, there is the person who has decided that their direction is to end their own life. If your direction is negative you can reverse it.

However, wandering is about a half hearted attempt to swim upstream with the only real determination being to stop being swept downstream. Someone who has taken a self-destructive course has decided to abandon all attempts to swim and allowed the current to take them where it wills. This need not be a conscious decision. It may just be a complete abandonment to what is seen to be inevitable. When someone believes that all their choices have been taken from them they will exercise one last choice to surrender to the downward pull of death.

In that respect I would say that wandering is infinitely preferable to the self destruct path, however there is a travelling companion that affects us all and if not identified and controlled, it will take us from Journeying to wandering, or from wandering to the suicide path. This is something I mentioned in Chapter 4—our self talk. If our self talk is telling us that what we are doing is pointless, or hopeless or silly or selfish or whatever it tries to drag us down with, we will end up stopping our pursuit and it will become a self-fulfilling prophecy.

Self talk is not wrong in itself. It will happen whether we like it or not. We just need to tame it and reprogram it to keep us on the path in the direction we choose rather than allowing it to take us off the path.

Once we have our direction sorted, and we are on the Journey once more there is something else waiting to hold us back. This is something I have already mentioned, called regrets.

Nostalgia and Regrets

· · · · · · · · · · · · · ·

"**REGRETS, I'VE HAD A FEW**, but then again, too few to mention," crooned Frank Sinatra in "My Way". Lucky man, if it was true! Most of us have more regrets than we care to mention. Regrets are usually associated with people who have been on the Journey of life. One exception is people who are still too young to have had regrets. I had them before I was nine. People who have lived perfect lives have no regrets. The rest of us real folks have to deal with them.

Regrets are associated with the 'should have', 'could have' and 'would have' moments in our lives. They are as pointless as they are many. There is nothing you can do about 'should have', 'could have', 'would have' other than learn from them not to make the same mistake the second time, or the third time or whatever. They are always about things in the past, usually way beyond our reach, and by that I mean more than a nanosecond ago.

We are creatures that make our Journey in something called Time. Time is a fascinating subject and endless volumes have been written on it. It passes by us at a steadily consistent rate of 60 seconds every minute and never pauses for breath. It has a direction (called 'Time's arrow') and it is definitely a one way affair! I know that a quantum physicist somewhere is going to take issue with me on that one, but for the intents and purposes of our Journey, it is one way.

It is like driving in a long tunnel like the ones under the Alps that go for miles. Except in the Time tunnel there is no reversing, no speeding up and no slowing down. You can check the rear vision mirror to see what has gone on before. You can even see a little way ahead, but you cannot affect the road you have just travelled or the road that is coming up. You just keep moving in the same direction.

We do, however, seem to leave markers behind in the tunnel. There are two kinds of marker that we use. Positive markers leave us with a memory of a good time in the past that we often long to return to. This is Nostalgia—the good old days. Quite often the memory is coloured in some way with a nice rosy tint that makes it seem better than it actually was at the time. This is not just a fond memory of some pleasant time. Nostalgia is linked with a nagging yearning to get back to that time.

The negative markers are linked to the memory of a time that we feel we need to hang on to as if we can somehow go back there and correct the mistake. No matter how much we tell ourselves that it's no point crying over spilt milk, we are still left with the longing to change the past, rather than just learn from it. That is what I mean by Regret.

To be fair, there is a third marker that we leave at times. That is when a bad thing happens that, with the passing of time, seems less bad and eventually makes a good story. These are usually more or less benign things that, while very inconvenient or even painful at the time, we get over and learn to laugh about.

This would include things like breaking a limb or a costly car wreck. As long is there is a good story to weave around it later, it leaves a rather familiar scar that we can smile about when we touch it.

The truly terrible thing about both Nostalgia and Regrets, however, is that they keep us tied to something that we no longer have access to, namely the past, in a way that is not at all helpful. It's as if we have an anchor linked to some point or points in the past, with a long cord that becomes ever longer, but never seems to break. Notwithstanding the fact that Time presses on regardless of these links, they still manage to hold us back from proceeding with our Journey.

Imagine yourself setting out on a ten mile hike. You have your boots on, your coat, your backpack with food, water, map and compass; you are ready to go! About 200 yards up the path you think, "Did I lock the car?" It nags at you for a while, and after another 20 yards you go back, check the car. It was locked. And off you go again. You make it to quarter of a mile this time, and you think, "Did I leave the lights on?" You turned a corner after the first 30 yards, so you'll have to go back to check. Sure enough, lights were off. Off you trot once more. Half a mile later, "Did I leave the sat nav on the dash?"

You get the idea. Being tied to your car like that you'll never get anywhere! As long as we are constantly revisiting the past either via Nostalgia or Regrets we tie ourselves up. That incredibly long cord I mentioned keeps us linked to the anchor of the memory marker that we made and we never truly move forward. We just get older. So let's have a look at the Regret words I have already mentioned.

"Would have" is usually loaded up with an "if". I would have done it if I had the money or the support or the intelligence or the nerve. Something I lacked or something that somebody else did or didn't do was responsible for me not doing it. The presence of the "would" however is the link with the past, the regret that holds us back, because usually the same "if" that stopped us last time is still there so it will be a "would have" again next time it comes up.

"Could have" is a guilty plea. I know that I was capable of it, but for some reason I chose not to. This one is probably the least excusable of the three, but the fact that I could have but didn't means I can't be relied on to do any differently in the future. A "could have" is a useless plea because the obvious response is "why didn't you then?" It's probably better just to keep my mouth shut.

"Should have" means that I am bound by guilt. It is less of a guilty plea, and more like a guilty plague. I know that it was the right thing to do it, but even so, it didn't get done so now I feel bad. It's not much different to "could have"; although it makes it sound like I care more about the failure, the same response is justified.

The common thing about all woulda, coulda, shoulda pleas is that they are all followed by "but". They all tie us to the past with regrets that nothing can be done about. The simple cure for all of these is to change them to a simple statement of fact. Instead of "I should have visited him before he died," it becomes "I didn't visit him before he died. End of. Now I am getting on with my life." Instead of "I could have done that better," try "I didn't do that well enough, I will do better next time." And for "I would have called you, but I didn't have the number," how about "Let me write down your number so next time I'll be able to call."

Regrets hold us back because we find ourselves constantly visiting places in our mind that we can never get to. There are people who need us to be present here and now doing things that we are perfectly capable of doing but we aren't doing because we stopped our Journey to keep revisiting a Regret. I'm not suggesting for one instant that we don't learn from the mistakes of the past. Look at the "would have" and say "what can I learn about what held me back?" For a "could have" ask yourself why you made a choice not to do what you were fully capable of doing. And for "should have" stop wallowing in self pity and decide that next time you will.

Of course there is a form of two of these that follows another regret clause, "if only". "If only so-and-so had happened, I could have . . ." and "If only I'd known, I would have . . .". This shows a desperate desire to rewrite the past a different way to create a different outcome. There is no "but" following these pleas, just a downcast expression that means we stop trying in those areas. The sheer futility of this is saddening. Why get bogged down in the "If only"? Whatever was required didn't happen, so there is nothing you can do.

Trying to live simultaneously in the past and the present is a lost cause. You will never alter the past or atone for what you did or didn't do. Carrying the guilt won't change anything and won't help anyone. And if it is nostalgia that keeps you tied up there, you may as well face that you will never recapture that moment. Even if you were to recreate the exact circumstances, you are different and so is everyone else that was involved.

There is nothing to stop you, however, from creating better moments in the future.

Where do we go from here on our Journey? Well, when it comes to the nostalgia, look at what it is you've been getting out of the trips back down memory lane. Since you'll never be able to recreate that moment again, what is the hunger that draws you back there and what are you going to create in the future that makes it worth your while moving forward? Nobody does anything unless they are getting something out of it and our nostalgia trips are feeding us in some way. If it is a relationship that was special, there are many relationships that can be created in the future. If it was a special time and place, there can be many more of those if we will stop clinging to the ones that have passed.

The sad thing is that the nostalgic moments of the past dull our appreciation of new experiences in the present moment. They are never good enough because they are constantly being compared to the unreachable but 'ideal' past experiences. If we will let them stand on their own merit, we'll find that they become new friends. As long as they are tainted by comparisons they will never measure up and so they'll never be satisfying.

As for our regrets, they are thieves that rob not only ourselves, but also the others who could benefit from what we are able to give if we are fully present in the here and now instead of tied into what would have, could have or should have been. There are people waiting for us to fully manifest what we are able to do if we will stop allowing regrets to tell us that we can't. Some of those people are our spouse, our children, people that we would never dream of stealing from. Yet we are blithely robbing them every day without a twinge of guilt.

What right do we have to simply wallow in our self pity and let the regrets of our past dictate what we do in the here and now and paint the picture of what our future is like? It's time to take your Journey as if today really was the very first day of your life. What would your Journey look like if none of those regrets had any power over you? Just think about the possibilities of what you could create if you didn't have a million reasons why you couldn't do them? Because that's what regrets do. They burden us down with all the excuses that we need to not do what we are meant to do.

I said with nostalgia that we don't do anything unless we are getting something out of it and it's the same with regrets. What we mostly get out of regrets is the convenient excuse to not try any more because the last time we tried we failed. Sometimes life is just so much more comfortable if we don't have to deal with those unhappy memories in a positive way. We can cuddle up to them, feed them, feed off them, but to have to give them up altogether so we can move on is too high a price to pay.

With no more excuses we can continue our Journey and do something that sounds too simple to be anything special—live in and for the now. As we Journey in this Time tunnel we can see behind and maybe a little ahead, but we can't live in either the past or the future. We can and must make plans for the future, but we'll never be able to go there any faster than 60 seconds per minute.

We only have one time that we can Journey in and that time is now. For many of us, now is boring or painful or sad or fearful. That's why we want to live in the past or rush to the future! But listen for a minute. What is happening right now?

Nothing you say? The reality is that there is never nothing happening. Your perception might be that nothing is going on, at least not anything that matters to you, but while you have been reading this paragraph, people have died, been born, gone broke, made a fortune.

If you have a child what are they doing right now? Do you even know? If you are married or have a significant other, what is he or she busy at while you are reading? As I have already mentioned in an earlier chapter, I realised not so long ago when I saw my grandchildren in church that as I was looking at one of them, they would never be like that again. If I didn't see them till next week as is usually the case, they would be a week older. What will I miss? What if they are ill next week and I don't see them?

When another of my grandchildren was with us the other day, I had things I really was supposed to be doing. But I went downstairs and suggested to my son that we three (my grandson, he and I) all go outside and kick a ball around. I still got my work done, but I spent a bit of quality time with two of my boys that I would have missed otherwise. Of course you've heard all this before, but a Journey is so much better if you do some sightseeing on the way.

So we come at last to the end of our Journey and the beginning of another as we enter the Departure Lounge, or at least some of us do.

Departure Lounge

· · · · · · · · · · · · ·

IT'S BEEN AN INTERESTING JOURNEY but as with all
Journeys it eventually comes to an end. As we've already
seen, some people try to find ways to make it go on forever,
but this Journey is not meant to do that. There a number
of crisis points that highlight the fact that the Journey is
not going to last forever. Maybe it's reaching fifty. Having
grandchildren can make you feel old. Having a parent or both
parents die of old age is definitely a clear reminder that our
own days are numbered. Then we reach something that we
call 'Retirement'.

Statistics tell us that men in particular tend not to live long after
they cease full time employment unless they have something
else planned to keep them occupied. That's because they no
longer have a purpose to keep them alive. They have simply
settled into the Departure Lounge and are expecting to die,
consciously or subconsciously.

The Departure Lounge is the place we get to in our Journey
where we have decided that we are in preparation for death.
Most people wouldn't admit it that bluntly, but that is the
reality. They have retired, life is just ordinary, their kids don't
visit, don't call, nothing else significant is going to happen
with their lives, they are just watching TV and waiting for the

inevitable. That is not to say that everyone in the Departure Lounge is going to die in the next few days. They may live for decades in the Departure Lounge, but in a sense, they are already dead.

I used to be the sort of person that gets to an Airport ready for the flight and wants to check in, get through passport control and security, sit in the seats at the gate and wait to be boarded. I'm still a bit that way if I let myself be, but now if there's time, I like to have a hot chocolate or browse the shops. I don't think I'll ever be like someone I know who likes to shop till the final boarding call and nearly misses her flight. But just sitting and waiting is so wasteful. Of course it helps that I have a wife who gets bored waiting to be boarded.

In the same way, getting into the Departure Lounge of life and simply waiting to die is such a shameful waste of a good life. For a start you have sixty plus years of experience to offer someone. That's not the time to shut down, that's the time to shine. Science is starting to tell us that, despite the ageing process, our brains keep on going till we die. The myth about brain cell deterioration and death after we reach 20 has been busted! The only reason many people deteriorate is that they just believe that they will.

Far from being the time to pack up your hiking gear and give up on your Journey, it's the time to get out and keep on living life to the full. Who can you help? Who can you cheer up? Who can you visit? Or, what about something you want to do for yourself? Is there something you never got around to doing? Even if there are long lists of things you feel you can't do there are probably still many things you can do.

One of the saddest stories I heard in recent times was the story of a man who wanted to end his life. He had an extraordinary amount of paralysis. His only way of communicating was by moving his eyes. He had to be bathed, fed, put to bed, dressed and otherwise cared for by others. He saw no point to living any longer. Yet despite all this, he used a computer to communicate using his eyes. A text-to-speech device gave him that ability to talk. He was quite articulate. It seemed such a waste to me that he wanted to deprive people of the opportunity to hear what he had to say.

I don't want to criticise him. I have not been in his shoes. He made his own choice and maybe he even got what he wanted. But he still had a choice, and that choice could have been to live as much as he was able, instead of the choice to die. Hopefully you are not at that extreme and the price you will pay for keeping on blessing us with your company on the Journey is not that high. We have so much to give one another as we Journey together that we need never consider ourselves as merely in life's departure lounge.

Having said all of that, there is, however, an element of preparation in our latter years, preparation that too few actually participate in. We've already mentioned this, but the question people seem least likely to want to address is "Where am I going when I die?" (Of course there is always someone who wants to know where they are going to die so they can avoid going there.) Now I don't recommend that you defer answering or at least addressing the question of where you are going until you are old and grey and sitting in the departure lounge, but if you are old and grey and you still haven't thought about it then it probably bears your consideration!

Speaking personally, I don't like to leave things to chance. If I am going to an event, I like to book travel, tickets and accommodation if necessary, in advance so I know that such things will be taken care of when I arrive. I'm not one for turning up at the airport and waiting around for a standby, arriving in a new city and hoping I find a hotel with a room free and turning up for a guided tour hoping that there is a spare slot for me! Yet many people treat life's Journey that way. They expect to kind of slip into the next life and hope that everything turns out OK.

The position I adopt is, you are by now abundantly clear on, the Christian point of view. I believe that not only is it possible to know what lies at the end of our Journey but that we have an active choice in what happens. It's not down to a lucky accident whether we have a good afterlife or a bad one. But whatever your world view is, the decision is pretty final. You can hope for reincarnation or some form of purgatory where you can redeem yourself if you like, but make up your mind quickly because soon it will be too late to make the choice!

I had a discussion with an atheist once in which he presented an impassioned argument for his position. He was not happy with the idea of we Christians having the uncertainty of faith. His view was that God did not exist and that when he died then he would no longer exist either. I pointed out to him that he actually had more faith than I did. When he asked why, I said to him that if he was right and I was wrong, then we would both cease to exist and that would be the end of both our Journeys, with nothing more to worry about. However if he was wrong and I was right, we would both meet our Maker and have to give account. He had a lot of faith that he was right if he was relying on that position! He admitted that I had a point.

I am not trying to make an apologetic for the existence of God; He already knows He exists. But from where I sit, the atheist is making a Journey to nowhere. If God really does not exist and there is no accounting then we may as well just do whatever we can get away with and enjoy as much as we can! Clinging on to any idea of morality while at the same time believing there is no God is pointless. The Apostle Paul put it that "if in this life only we have hope in Christ, we (the Christians) are of all men the most pitiable." And he also says "If the dead do not rise, 'Let us eat and drink, for tomorrow we die!'"

I never did like the idea of going nowhere so when I met the Man on the Tree I found that I could not only have both hope and faith, but I could know where I was Journeying to. Or, as I have already suggested, Who I was Journeying to. That's why I can afford to spend time browsing in the shops, or sitting having a hot chocolate. I don't need to rush to the departure lounge and sit waiting for my flight. I'll know when the boarding call comes and I won't miss my flight. What's more, I know where my flight is headed.

Growing old is a state of mind as much as it is a state of body. There are people who die young, very late in life and there are people who die old, very early in life. If you are one of the latter, you can help yourself by making the decision now to stop growing older. I detest jokes about the ageing process. They do nothing but negatively reinforce the stereotype that we will lose our hair, our teeth, our memories, our vigour, our passion and that we are on an inevitable downhill Journey. Why would you want to make fun of that?

Instead, why not make your latter years the best years of your life? What is the reason that you just accept the received wisdom? My wife's grandfather was 90-something when he died, and the carers in the home he was in wanted to stop him from eating certain things that were 'bad' for him. I figured that at his age he had earned the right to eat what he wanted to and die happy! He knew where he was going and wanted to live life to the end. Of course they got their way, but I think it was a shame. Someone I know has a grandmother who is over 110 and she refuses to grow old, but preaches to everyone around her in a care home.

So what's it going to be at the end of your Journey? Head for the departure lounge as soon as you can and sit down to Sudoku? Or decide that the Journey isn't over till it's over? Who knows what amazing things you can accomplish? Just think: if you retired at 65 and lived to 90, that's a quarter of a century to both get and give value from. What a long time to sit in front of the TV and snarl at the weatherman!

Of course you may have physical difficulties. I don't deny that that is a very real possibility. But if you focus on what you can do instead of dwelling on what you can't do you will find that life can still be amazing. This is nothing to do with old age. Someone who is physically restricted in some way can be as 'old' as someone who is advanced in years. If we let our body's limitations rob us of our future then we are losing out. Everyone's body is restricted. I can't fly because I don't have wings but I don't notice that because no-one else does either, so I do what I can within the laws of physics. If you don't have the use of your legs or if you are missing a limb, if everyone else was the same you'd think nothing of it and get on with life.

Finally, the boarding call comes. "Will passenger Chris Tingle please come to the departure lounge? Your flight is ready for immediate departure." And when I cross over into the next life, I am going to find yet another Garden and yet another Tree.

Under a Tree (finale)

* * * * * * * * * * * * *

IMAGINE MY LIFE'S JOURNEY IS over. I have crossed the line into the next world. I don't know what it is like other than that to be absent from the body is to be present with the Lord. So I expect the first sight I will have is the face of Jesus. He is the destination of my Journey, after all! I have pictured the moment often. I'll have my little book of questions ready, all set to ask Him to settle life's puzzles once and for all. Then as I look into His smiling face, I'll smile right back, throw the book over my shoulder, and rush to Him for an embrace that will encompass my whole life.

However I know that there is a City in the new earth, and if there is a City then there will be another Journey, and one day I will stand in that City. The amazing thing about this City is that it is an enormous cube 1500 miles to a side! So it would be quite a Journey just to get to the middle of it. The Throne of God is in the City and while it doesn't say where in the City it is, I'd imagine it would be round about the middle. From the Throne of God there flows a river, and on either side of the river grows a variety of Tree. The variety of tree is the Tree of Life. Adam and Eve stood near that Tree, but focused instead on another Tree, the one under which they chose death instead of life. I stood there with them because they were my oldest ancestors.

Then I stood under another Tree and received forgiveness from the Lamb of God. Finally I will stand under the Tree of Life in what must be a Garden, because there is a river and there are trees growing there. Finally I will have returned to the source of Life that Adam and Eve and the whole of Mankind lost access to millennia ago. And as I continue on my Journey meeting who knows who along the way, travelling with some truly amazing people, just like you have been for Journeying with me this far, I will eat of that Tree forever. And this Journey truly will last for eternity.

Once again, we have been confused about our destination being a Place rather than a Person. The Grand Plan of God for our Journey is for His family to be reunited. As many of us who choose the Tree of Life rather than the tree of death will be united together will continue together in that eternal Journey—no painful prolongation of this life, but stepping into the Journey that we were always meant to be on.

So one day I hope to see your face, learn your name, and rejoice with you in your Journey, either the one in this world or the one in the next. Until then, Bon Voyage!

About the Author

⸿ ⸿ ⸿ ⸿ ⸿ ⸿ ⸿ ⸿ ⸿ ⸿ ⸿ ⸿ ⸿

CHRIS BEGAN HIS JOURNEY IN Sheffield, England and moved with his parents and brother to Brisbane, Australia in 1965. After thirty years of living and travelling in Australia, he returned to England with his wife, Desley, and six children to start a new life in a country he barely remembered. Eleven grandchildren later, He lives in Swindon, the former hub of many Journeys on the Great Western Railway. He has travelled extensively in Europe and has visited the USA several times, as well as the Ukraine and Israel. In the UK he has done a fair bit of hiking and has climbed to the top of the famous `three peaks', Scafell Pike, Snowdon and Ben Nevis.

In 2009 he and Desley began a very different Journey with the aid of an organisation called Klemmer and Associates—a Journey of self-discovery. He is now a graduate of all the courses provided by K & A and has discovered that, in a very real way, Life is a Journey that we are all involved in even if we've never set foot out of our own town. Now he has written a book that he hopes will help inspire and encourage fellow travellers as he shares insights he has gained into aspects of Life's Journey, as they join with him and see it through fresh eyes.